52 Romantic Outings in Greater Cleveland

"Carey has assembled and detailed dates sure to entice first-time couples and seasoned lovers alike."
—*The Plain Dealer*

"How can you pitch your woo on [Valentine's] day and the rest of the year? Miriam Carey answers that question with originality and humor." —*Free Times*

"The recipes are far from traditional, but they're sure to spark romance."—*The News-Herald*

"Gives the romantic heart that beats somewhere inside all of us inspiration to keep the Valentine's Day spirit year 'round.... It can be shared by two people who've just met or by a couple celebrating their 20th anniversary."—*Call & Post*

"Great little book! Start this week and try all 52."
—WZJM FM

Fifty-two
ROMANTIC
OUTINGS
in Greater
CLEVELAND

Miriam Carey

GRAY & COMPANY, PUBLISHERS
CLEVELAND

Gray & Company, Publishers
1588 E. 40th Street
Cleveland, Ohio 44103
(216) 431-2665
www.grayco.com

ISBN 1-886228-21-3

This guide was prepared on the basis of the author's best knowledge at the time of publication. However, because of constantly changing conditions beyond the author's control, the author disclaims any responsibility for the accuracy and completeness of the information in this guide. Users of this guide are cautioned not to place undue reliance upon the validity of the information contained herein and to use this guide at their own risk.

Printed in the United States of America

10 9 8 7 6 5 4 3 2

Contents

Acknowledgments

Many times my brothers, sisters, and I would sit around the kitchen table complaining about the lack of romance in our lives. "Oh, it's out there," my mother would say, ever so slightly annoyed, "you just have to look for it!"

Well, Mom, I went out looking, and here's my detailed report.

Encouragement was the key factor in writing this book. Thanks go first to Rich Osborne for encouraging me to pitch it and next to David Gray and Mike Morgenstern for encouraging me to pitch it again. The raw energy and enthusiasm of tireless Jane Lassar and Karen Fuller encouraged me to keep writing. Continual encouragement came in the form of phone calls and e-mails from such friends as Jerry Fragapane, James Powell, Kathleen Carey, Denise Dufala, and Anna Vedouras, each of whom happily answered strange questions in the middle of the night without hesitation. Each also showed a shrewd understanding of the crucial difference between the phrases, "How's it coming?" and "Is it done yet?" The support mechanism of an unusually large, caring, and dedicated group of friends and family that I look to for inspiration includes the First Friday gang, as well as Ellen Stein Burbach, P. J. Bednarski, Tom Feran, John McCann, all of my brothers and sisters, and the original members of the LSB. Thanks also to Jack, who helped with the turnaround.

All those who contributed to this book are quoted within its pages wherever possible. Clevelanders are a rare and proud breed who brag humbly about their creations, businesses, and ideas while putting forth intense effort to serve wonderful food, sell fascinating products, and provide invaluable services. Patronize the many small businesses mentioned in this book, for at these shops you pay for products, but you also purchase the continued success and personalized service of such ventures.

Certain couples contributed invaluably to the spirit of this book simply by being so much in love. They include each of my aunts and uncles, Mike and Shannon Dolan, Pete and Ellen Kwiatkowski, and above and beyond all others, Walter and Lucille Carey. I am also grateful to those strong women who taught me so very much—Margaret, Eileen, and Kay—and the Sweeney sisters who keep alive the old stories and traditions. And, of course, a tip of the hat to the Irish Muse who visits every so often.

Finally, heaps of thanks to Gavin for his unique perspective, unconditional encouragement, and great gales of laughter.

INTRODUCTION

*m*y friends don't know about it. Neither does my family. It's something I try to keep under wraps as best I can, and hope that no one will notice. If they found out, it might damage my reputation.

I can't have everyone in town knowing that I'm a hopeless romantic.

When I decided to write this book, my friends laughed. "You? Miriam? A book about romantic places to go?" I guess that my track record with dates and boyfriends—a frighteningly long losing streak of wanna-be's and ne'er-do-wells—makes them think that I'm not the most qualified person to pontificate on the many hidden romantic treasures of Cleveland. But they're wrong.

For the last two years I've been annoying people with invasive questions. At a wedding, I'd throw out to the table, "Do you believe in true love?" At a bar with friends, I'd query, "Where do you think Cleveland's romantic epicenter is?" Over drinks with a new friend I'd prod, "Do you remember where you were the very last time you felt the beginnings of true romantic love?" Most of the time they answered honestly. Sometimes, they'd blush. But always—after the conversation had died down—I'd catch them drifting off in a romantic revery.

I live in a secret world, drifting through downtown daydreaming about my fantasy Cleveland. There, the Avenue is still the Terminal Tower, and I'm a lady in a silk suit with a matching hat, handbag, shoes, and gloves waving good-bye to my true love as he boards the train to serve in WWII. On my jaunt down Euclid Avenue there is always a gentleman under the arch of the Arcade peering eagerly toward Public Square anticipating my arrival, tipping his felt hat and rearranging the folds of his trench coat. And when I travel to the country, I know I'll be treated to a hayride through an apple orchard so pungent with the scent of fall that I'll have no choice but to slide into the arms of the tall, dark, and handsome fellow next to me for a long, warm kiss.

But this is the real world, and these are modern times. So I set out to write this book knowing I could uncover some of Cleveland's hidden treasures and share them with other hopeless romantics like myself. Together, I thought, we could share the bustle of Public Square, the glory of the blooming countryside, and the endless charms that await us in the little nooks and crannies of this town of ours. I envision a city full of happy couples walking hand in hand down the city streets, their hearts filled with love, copies of *Fifty-two Romantic Outings in Greater Cleveland* tucked under their arms for reference.

Yes, this is the Cleveland of my dreams. A town so full of love that its borders can barely contain it. The shores of Lake Erie teaming with lip-locked lovers at sunset, the country roads just outside of town bursting with picnickers on their way to little hideaways for a Saturday afternoon.

In each chapter, you'll find an itinerary for an outing or date in greater Cleveland. Some outings are simple, others are more complicated. Some require a big budget, others little more than the cost of a few gallons of gas. Use the book as you like. Choose a different chapter every week for an entire year, and you'll have something new to do each week, or refer to the book periodically for an idea, or an answer to that gnawing question: "What's something we can do that's different?" Parachuting over the farmlands of Northeast Ohio might be just the cure for that dinner-and-a-movie rut you're in.

My friends, ever the smart alecks, point out that even after spending two years researching and writing on the topic of romance, I still haven't found any for myself. They're wrong again. True romance isn't to be found in a mate, or even a place. It's in your heart. And what you make of it is up to you.

Fifty-two
ROMANTIC
OUTINGS
in Greater
CLEVELAND

Key to the Data

Time. About how long it will take you to do the whole date as I've presented it.

Season. What time of year you can go on the outing. Usually has to do with weather, but sometimes has to do with availability.

Location. What part of town you'll visit to do the outing. Often I've included variations for a similar outing in a different part of town.

Season: Spring, Fall, Winter
Time: 4 hours ~ **Location:** East
Intimacy level: 1 ~ **Cost:** $$$
Advance planning: Some

Intimacy Level. Suggests how well the two of you should probably know each other in order to feel comfortable on the date. Any outing can be tailored to fit any relationship, but the outings as I present them fit best into these intimacy level ratings.

1 = Good for first dates and good friends.

2 = Best for couples who know each other pretty well and at least have serious intentions.

3 = For long-term relationships and married couples.

(Of course, if you're comfortable enough to go on an outing rated "3," you can certainly handle a "1.")

Cost is an estimate of how much you'll probably need to spend on this date:

$ = Free–$20
$$ = $21–$50
$$$ = $51–$80
$$$ = $80 and more

Advance Planning. Can we just pick up and go? Do we need reservations? Do I schedule way ahead?

None = No planning. You can pick up and do these outings at a moment's notice.

Some = Plan a day or two in advance to make diner reservations, check a show schedule, or reserve a seat.

A Lot = Plan well in advance to do things like order tickets, book a hotel room, or reserve a special day and time.

Outing 1

A FOOLPROOF NIGHT UNDER THE STARS

Season: Spring, Fall, Winter
Time: 4 hours ~ **Location:** East
Intimacy level: 1 ~ **Cost:** $$$
Advance planning: Some

What You'll Do

❧ Pick up a couples astrological chart at Delphic Books ($20).

❧ Stargaze at the Cleveland Museum of Natural History observatory (admission $6.50 per person).

❧ Dine under the stars on the patio (by the window) at That Place on Bellflower ($35–$60 per couple).

❧ Continue the evening under the stars on the patio of the Barking Spider for after-dinner drinks ($10–$15 per couple).

NOTE: *You'll need to pick a Wednesday night between September and May, when the observatory at the Cleveland Museum of Natural History is open to the public. At least a day before, call Delphic Books to order your couples astrological chart. The morning you'd like to go, check the weather forecast for clear skies in the evening (216-931-1212).*

*B*rilliant starry nights are the stuff of which romance is made—and the inspiration for many famous musical works, from the corny "Harvest Moon" to the very sultry "Midnight Sun" (the Ella Fitzgerald version from the Songbook series will give you goose bumps). Beautiful, inspiring, humbling—the night sky is all this and more, especially when the view is shared with a loved one. Stargazing is made easy in Cleveland's University Circle, where the Museum of Natural History provides a dome-covered observatory and even houses its own night sky under cover of its planetarium. You'll visit there this evening for an up-close encounter with the universe.

Step by Step

9 A.M. THE DAY BEFORE YOU GO: Place a phone call to Delphic Books and order a couples astrological chart; let them know you plan to pick it up at around 7:30 p.m. (charts take an hour or two to compile). Have handy the day, month, year, and time of birth for both you and your date. Delphic will prepare a printed astrological chart that describes your individual characteristics and also your traits as a pair. "The chart interprets relationships using data from two individuals," says Delphic owner, Lori Brdar. "It defines what each individual is looking for in a relationship and compares data for compatibility." The charts include detailed descriptions of how the planets were aligned when each of you was born, and how this alignment will affect your destinies as individuals and as a pair. The couples chart costs $20. One printout per couple.

7:30 P.M. THE DAY OF YOUR DATE: Stop by Delphic to pick up your chart, pocket it without peeking, and keep it handy for reference after your trip to the observatory. While you're here, browse around. Brdar says her store has one of the largest astrology sections in the city and carries everything from books for the novice astrologer to advanced materials for the more savvy astronomical enthusiast. Among the eclectic mix you might find a guidebook to help stimulate your new interest in the heavens. (Delphic closes at 8 p.m.)

8:30 P.M.: Arrive at the Cleveland Museum of Natural History Ralph Mueller Planetarium and Observatory. This is one of Cleveland's hidden gems, and great pains have been taken to preserve its place in this community. Even as observatories in other cities are dismantled because of poor funding and light pollution, Mueller has been kept viable by University Circle's installation of special streetlights that shine downward only, allowing for a clearer view of the sky above.

The observatory is the perfect perch for viewing a clear sky. Its ceiling can be retracted slightly to allow the 10.5-inch refracting telescope a clear view of objects in space. The telescope—made right here in Cleveland 100 years ago by Warner & Swasey—swivels to provide highly magnified views of different areas of the night sky, taking in the moon, stars, and planets. "Depending on what time of year it is, you can see Jupiter's four largest moons, jewel-like star clusters, and double solar systems," says observatory coordinator Clyde Simpson.

Simpson or one of his associates will welcome you to the observatory with a brief description of its history and purpose, and of the equipment housed there. During your visit you and a handful of other visitors will be invited to take turns looking through the eyepiece of the telescope at various parts of the sky. Because the telescope can move up, down, back, and forth, you'll get to see a cross-section of the hemisphere above Cleveland. Throughout the course of the evening—the observatory is open until 10 p.m.—there will be plenty of opportunities to see major sights in the night sky.

...planets jockey for position in the darkness, and a simulated shooting star or two seem to fall from the ceiling into your lap.

Of course, this being Cleveland, there are evenings when all you'll get from the telescope is a clear view of murky clouds, even if the morning weather report foretold clear skies. That's where the planetarium comes in handy. Its circular lobby features displays of meteorites and an interesting array of antique instruments (dating back to a time when an inaccurate reading of the skies could cost you your earthly skin if you were a sailor or a desert traveler dependent on the stars for your course). Inside the planetarium, the Hanna Star Dome seems to float overhead, the setting for complex, fiber-optic planetarium shows. During a typical show, the dome, which provides an accurate picture of the night sky, rotates to show the changing seasons astrally. Programs take about a half-hour, as the night sky changes from month to month, planets jockey for position in the darkness, and a simulated shooting star or two seem to fall from the ceiling onto your lap.

Whether the stars you see this evening are fiber-optic replicas or the real thing, you'll be humbled by your celestial experience.

By now, you're probably hungry, too.

10 P.M.: A 10-minute walk or 5-minute drive will take you to That Place on Bellflower. Set back from Bellflower Road, this century-old converted carriage house and stable now features all the comfort of a cozy country home. And, more importantly, you'll get a fabulous view of the night sky from the private patio in the back of the restaurant or, in colder weather, from a window seat indoors.

Low lighting, plenty of candles, and a fireplace enhance the warmth and charm here. The menu cleverly mixes such contemporary creations as escargot in champagne butter with comforting standards like Beef Wellington. Place an order and settle in for dinner. Now is a good time to bring out the couples chart you picked up earlier.

Astrological charts can strike you one of two ways: as complete bunk or as a celestial revelation focused solely on you. Either way, it's fun to read through the chart, comparing your traits. Astrological charts can function as ice-breakers for new couples, supplying plenty of fodder for conversation; or they can be refresher courses for more settled-in pairs, providing an opportunity to vent through the innocuous grouping of traits the charts provide. By the time you order your after-dinner cappuccino, the stars will have new meaning for you.

11:30 P.M.: Still enchanted? Slip through the alley just behind That Place on Bellflower to the Barking Spider Tavern, where another patio beckons starry-eyed lovers. This club—also a converted stable—offers a rustic brand of homeyness. Bric-a-brac adorns the walls, a mishmash of tables and chairs beckons you to take a seat, and the beer coolers contain a wide variety of beer and wine. Local musicians frequently play at the Barking Spider in front of mellow but interested small crowds. On any given night you can hear folk, rock, or blues. To maintain the focus of this evening, take a seat outside on the patio and let the music drift out to you, turning your head upward every so often to look at the starry, starry sky. (To avoid seeing the wrong kinds of stars, limit your beer consumption appropriately; the Barking Spider is well known for its selection of strong, hearty brews.)

Complete your celestial evening with one last good night to the sky, one last hopeful look for a shooting star to wish on. Then count your lucky stars together. They're the ones that really matter.

Variations

WEST SIDERS: The Schuele Planetarium at the Metroparks Lake Erie Nature and Science Center at the Huntington Reservation opens after dark on the first and third Saturday of every month. Visit the night sky at the planetarium then dine just up the road at the Cabin Club, a rustic Western Reserve–style log cabin replica built in 1947. The Cabin Club prides itself on fresh, high-quality steaks (in fact, they'll let you pick the steak you want when they roll the steak cart to your table at ordering time), perfectly grilled big-game fish, and salmon. After dinner, make your way back to the Huntington Reservation for a firsthand view of the moon and stars over Lake Erie.

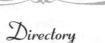

Directory

Barking Spider Tavern

11310 Juniper Rd., Cleveland

216-421-2863

HOURS/AVAILABILITY:
Tue–Fri 2 p.m.–1 a.m.;
Sat 4 p.m.–1 a.m.;
Sun 3 p.m.–12 a.m.

Cabin Club

30651 Detroit Rd., Westlake

440-899-7111

HOURS/AVAILABILITY:
Mon–Fri 11 a.m.–10:30 p.m.;
Sat noon–11:30 p.m.;
Sun 4 p.m.–10 p.m.

Cleveland Museum of Natural History

1 Wade Oval Drive, Cleveland

800-317-9155

HOURS/AVAILABILITY:
Clear Wednesday evenings
September–May until 10 p.m.

Delphic Books

1793 Coventry Rd., Cleveland Heights

216-321-8106

HOURS/AVAILABILITY:
Mon–Fri 10 a.m.–8 p.m.;
Sat 10 a.m.–7 p.m.;
Sun 1 p.m.–5 p.m.

Schuele Planetarium at the Lake Erie Nature and Science Center

28728 Wolf Rd., Bay Village

440-871-2900

HOURS/AVAILABILITY:
2nd and 4th Saturday of the month; call ahead; planetarium programs at 2 p.m. and 7 p.m.

That Place on Bellflower

11401 Bellflower Road, Cleveland

216-231-4469

HOURS/AVAILABILITY:
Mon 11:30 a.m.–3 p.m., Tue –Thu 11:30 a.m.–3 p.m. and 5:30 p.m.–9 p.m., Fri–Sat 5:30 p.m.–10 p.m., Sun 5 p.m.– 8:30 p.m.

Outing 2

A SLEIGH RIDE TOGETHER

Season: Winter ~ **Time:** 3 hours
Location: Far East
Intimacy level: 1 ~ **Cost:** $–$$$
Advance planning: Some

What You'll Do

🏹 Shop for snow gear in charming Chesterland ($20–$50).

🏹 Dash through the snow in a sleigh at Patterson Farms ($100 for up to 15 people; $250 with use of sugarhouse).

🏹 Play games, sip on cider, and lounge by the fireplace at the Patterson's old-fashioned sugarhouse.

NOTE: *At least 15 inches of snow must be on the ground in Chesterland for operation of this sleigh. Call ahead to make a reservation for a Saturday or Sunday sleigh ride at Patterson Farms (no rides after February 15). If you like, pack up a board game to play by the fire after the ride.*

For Santa, it's work, for Iditarod competitors it's survival. For the two of you, it's pure fun. A sleigh ride is among the charms of winter in northeastern Ohio. In the days of the early settlers, sleighs were the primary mode of wintertime transportation. Families bundled up to go to church on a Sunday with hot potatoes in their pockets for warmth. These days, sleigh rides are a charming dash through the past.

For our purposes, a sleigh ride is an inventive way to get close in the wintertime. Be sure to cuddle, and you can make believe—at least for the moment—that winter ain't so bad after all.

Even recreational sleigh rides, though, are becoming history, because sleighs are difficult to build and maintain. Also, the litigious nature of our current society threatens this treasured mode of transportation, as the family farmer who used to offer sleigh rides (a romantic way to subsidize the off-season) faces ever-higher insurance premiums. Say a silent word of thanks to the sleigh owners of today—die-hard romantics who refuse to cave in to the harsh realities of these modern times.

Step by Step

4 P.M.: Arrive in downtown Chesterland to browse through the charming shops. Pick up some warm mittens, a scarf, or a hat at Ferdl Aster Ski Shop (they also offer an assortment of outdoor gear for winter sports). Leave about 15 minutes to get to Patterson Farms. (Drive west on SR 6/Chardon Rd. to SR 306. Turn left onto SR 306. At next intersection, turn left onto Mulberry Road, Patterson Farms is 0.5 mile down on your right.)

5 P.M.: Arrive at Patterson Farms. Nancy and Jim Patterson—the fifth generation of Pattersons to run the farm—have crafted a bobsled in its original splendor. "The 'bob'," says Nancy Patterson, "is the old-fashioned runner that glides over the snow. We built a body for the sled based on traditional bobsleds." Add the Pattersons' two Percheron draft horses with their requisite bells jingling through the

In the wintertime the strawberry patches
rest under quilts of snow,
while icicles dangle their daggers
from the branches of apple trees.

crisp winter air, and you'll swear Norman Rockwell once painted this nostalgic winterscape.

The Pattersons' big sleigh holds up to 15 people, and Nancy Patterson believes that the distinctive romance of this adventure is best experienced by a group of friends, couples, or a family. The half-hour or so you'll spend on the sleigh provides plenty of time for storytelling and togetherness.

Your sleigh ride will take you on a wintry tour of the Pattersons' property via a path through orchards of bare apple trees. In the gentler seasons, the farm is a great place for strawberry-picking and cider-pulling. In the wintertime, however, the strawberry patches rest under quilts of snow, while icicles dangle their daggers from the branches of the apple trees.

5:45 P.M.: After your ride through this enchanted forest, warm up at the Pattersons' sugarhouse, designed for maple syrup production. This rustic room features a large fireplace and a lounging area where you can relax, sip on hot chocolate or cider, and play games if you brought them. It's bring-your-own at the sugarhouse, but you can stay as long as you like.

"We have couples who have come here for years," says Nancy, "and now some grandparents even bring their children. We believe in sharing what you have with others and love to invite people here to enjoy our land." Besides being enchanted by the Pattersons' lovely woods, you'll certainly be charmed by their homespun philosophy.

Variations

SLEIGHS ON THE HOMESTEAD: At Lake Farmpark one foot of snow is required for a proper sleigh ride, but the ride is worth waiting for. The two-seater sleigh is sleek, fast, and thrilling. You'll need to call at the beginning of the season; when the snow starts to fall, they'll give you a call. Rides are $35. On December weekends, this farm hosts the Country Lights Festival. More than 500,000 lights twinkle in the moonlight and cast shadows on snowy Kirtland. During the festival you can enjoy a candlelight dinner, tour a bevy of decorated trees, and watch the classic toy trains as they chug along. Sleigh rides continue after the holiday season, without the candlelight dinners. Instead, guests are invited for cocoa and sweets at the park's cafeteria.

THE OTHER NORTHFIELD PARK: Sleigh rides come with a historical message when you travel with the Carriage Trade. This horse-drawn sleigh ride through a family farm in the Cuyahoga Valley includes an oral history of the area by your driver/tour guide as you zip along—from the Ice Age to modern times. Afterwards, you're invited to warm up by a wood-burning stove, sip on cappuccino, and nibble on sweets in the "Sleigh Chalet." Cost is $60 per couple, $100 for two couples. Deposit required.

Directory

Carriage Trade
8050 Brandywine Rd., Northfield
330-467-9000

HOURS/AVAILABILITY:
All winter long
(weather permitting) Thu–Sun 1 p.m.–9 p.m.
Call for reservation.

Ferdl Aster Ski Shop
8330 Mayfield Rd., Chesterland
440-729-9472

HOURS/AVAILABILITY:
Mon–Fri 10 a.m.–8 p.m.,
Sat 10 a.m.–5 p.m.,
Sun 1 p.m.–5 p.m. Closed mid-Apr through Aug 1.

Lake Farmpark
8800 Chardon Rd., Kirtland
800-366-3276

HOURS/AVAILABILITY:
Tue–Thu and Sat–Sun 9 a.m.–2:30 p.m.
(weather and staff availability permitting). Call at beginning of season for reservation.

Patterson Farms
8765 Mulberry Rd., Chesterland
440-729-9809

HOURS/AVAILABILITY:
Sleigh rides Mid-Dec through mid-Feb
(weather permitting), Fri evening, Sat, and Sun.
Call for reservation.

Outing 3
AN ELABORATELY ROMANTIC LUNCH DATE

Season: Spring, Summer, Fall
Time: 1.5–2 hours ~ **Location:** Downtown
Intimacy level: 1 ~ Cost: $$–$$$
Advance planning: Some

What You'll Do

🌢 On a sunny day, pick up a picnic basket ($20–$40).

🌢 Meet your date and board a carriage at Public Square.

🌢 Have lunch at Willard Park.

NOTE: *You'll need to call Colonial Carriage at least 24 hours in advance to secure carriage and route for outing ($35/half hour).*

here is perhaps no greater threat to the romantic spirit than stress. It pervades modern life. Our hectic work schedules are already dragging into the evening, and chipping away at our weekends. It was recently reported on National Public Radio that the average American now spends only 14 minutes on lunch—often at his or her own desk. We need to offset all of that work time with some leisurely indulgence. How about breaking free from stress in the middle of the day with a perfectly decadent long lunch? Think of it as a fabulous way to collect comp time for all those 14-minute lunch breaks. It's also a fine way to spend some needed time with your loved one.

You could easily pick up a styrofoam lunch from a fast-food joint and eat outside. But for this outing, you'll want to go all out: midweek picnic full of romance and splendor in the grass. Remember that the secret to this kind of self-indulgence is to enjoy yourself, and enjoy the one you're with. Leave your pager, your cell phone, and your briefcase behind, and focus on having fun for a very long hour. You'll feel so refreshed, you'll want to make this a regular event.

Step by Step

A DAY—OR EVEN TWO—BEFORE THE EVENT: Check the weather forecast for sunny skies. Next, call Colonial Carriage. This is the company that pulls the horse-drawn, Cinderella-inspired rig through the streets of downtown. Owner Dave Nev is a romantic himself, having left his job as an engineer to start the business. "I wanted to bring some nostalgia back into the city," says Nev. Schedule a pick-up time and place for the next day. Rides usually go by the half hour and cost $35 per couple.

11:30 A.M., DAY OF PICNIC: Arrange for lunch. Pick up all you need to fill a picnic basket at Reserve Square Food Market in the Reserve Square building. Keep it simple: A loaf of fresh bread with soft, smoked Gouda cheese to go with it. Load up on some pasta salad from the deli, ruby red apples, seedless grapes, and sparking juice. Fresh pastries from the bakery include oversized cookies and moist cakes. Don't forget to pick up some plates, napkins, knives, and forks, too.

As the victorian carriage clatters an unfamiliar "clippety-clop" all the way down Euclid Avenue, the two of you can rest easy on the cushioned, plush velvet seats inside.

12 NOON: Meet your date in front of Terminal Tower. Have the carriage waiting nearby to surprise him or her. Arrange with the driver to pass through Public Square and Playhouse Square—the long route to Willard Park. As the Victorian carriage clatters an unfamiliar "clippety-clop" all the way down Euclid Avenue, the two of you can rest easy on the cushioned, plush velvet seats inside. Sit back and relax while the workday traffic whizzes by—you're enjoying your lunch break.

12:15 P.M.: Have Nev's carriage drop you off (and arrange for a pick-up time) by Claes Oldenburg's whimsical *Free Stamp* sculpture at Willard Park (next to city hall at Lakeside and East 9th). From there, you'll have a view of the lake and the Rock and Roll Hall of Fame and Museum. Linger over your lunch, taking in the view as boats and planes pass by. Look up at the sky and find pictures in the clouds ... indulge.

1 P.M.: Step into the carriage for the trip back to Public Square. This time, request a different route—down Lakeside Avenue and through the Warehouse district, perhaps. At Public Square, part with a kiss.

Variations

RAIN DELAY: In Cleveland, it never hurts to have a back-up plan. If the skies threaten rain, you have the option of lunching indoors in one of Cleveland's fantastic atriums. These ornate halls, bedecked with fauna and fountains, can breathe new life into a winter day or offer a pleasant refuge from an unexpected summer storm. The Van Sweringen Arcade at Landmark Office Towers is a stunningly romantic space to have a relaxing lunch if you're into art deco and things antique. Bring along a cobb salad that you can get to-go from the Hard Rock Cafe in Tower City, just across the street from Landmark Office Towers. Topped with ham, hard-boiled eggs, cheese, and bacon, this fresh salad is a colorful, healthy treat to share on a gray day.

SUBURBAN PICNIC SPOTS: Working in the suburbs? Here's a list of favorite picnic spots to help you escape the office park for an hour or so:

ROCKY RIVER: Pick up a thick deli sandwich at Lehman's Deli, then hop in the car and head for Clague Park at the intersection of Clague and Hilliard. Ducks wade lazily through the pond and sometimes approach for a crumb of bread (don't feed them until you're ready to leave, or you'll never get rid of them).

INDEPENDENCE: Get a lunch to go at Zayda's Deli, then picnic by the canal locks on the Towpath Trail in the Cuyahoga Valley National Recreation Area, at Rockside and Canal roads in Independence.

UNIVERSITY HEIGHTS: Get a gooseliver sandwich or corned beef stacked high at Corky & Lenny's, one of Cleveland's favorite delis.

Directory

Colonial Carriage
4323 Brooklyn Ave., Cleveland
216-459-1519
HOURS/AVAILABILITY:
Call to schedule ride.

Corky & Lenny's
27091 Chagrin Blvd.,
Woodmere
216-464-3838
HOURS/AVAILABILITY:
Sun–Thu 7:30 a.m.–11:30 p.m., Fri–Sat 7:30 a.m.–midnight

Hard Rock Cafe
230 W. Huron Rd., Cleveland
216-830-7625
HOURS/AVAILABILITY:
Sun–Thu 11 a.m.–11 p.m.,
Fri–Sat 10 a.m.–midnight

Lehman's Deli
24961 Detroit Rd., Westlake
440-871-3445
HOURS/AVAILABILITY:
Mon–Fri 8 a.m.–8 p.m.,
Sat 9 a.m.–4 p.m., Sun closed

Reserve Square Food Market
1701 E. 12th St., Cleveland
216-696-1012
HOURS/AVAILABILITY:
Mon–Fri 8 a.m.–7 p.m.,
Sat 9 a.m.–7 p.m.;
Sun noon–6 p.m.

Van Sweringen Arcade at Landmark Office Towers
101 Prospect, Cleveland
216-696-7400
HOURS/AVAILABILITY:
7:30 a.m.–7:30 p.m.

Zayda's Deli
6080 Brecksville Rd., Independence
216-642-4341
HOURS/AVAILABILITY:
Mon–Sat 11 a.m.–9 p.m.

Outing 4
POETRY SLAM

Season: Spring, Summer, Fall, Winter
Time: 3 hours ~ **Location:** Downtown/East
Intimacy level: 2 ~ **Cost:** $–$$
Advance planning: Some–a lot

What You'll Do

- Pick up supplies and inspiration at the Writing Room ($10–$40).
- Share poetry in the park.
- Attend a poetry reading.

NOTE: *Keep an eye out for poetry readings in the local papers, or subscribe to the Poets' League of Greater Cleveland mailing list to find out where readings are held each month.*

hether in the form of short love notes left casually around the house or an epic poem describing your love, poetry is a challenging way to express your feelings. Give it a try. The truly grand thing about poetry is its accessibility. You don't have to be Lord Byron or William Shakespeare to delight another with words. All it takes is a little bit of honesty, a little bit of time, and, well, a rhyming dictionary never hurts. Love poems are lasting pledges of your true feelings, and let's face it: they're much less expensive than diamonds.

Now, we're not talking about "pick up a gallon of milk—love you!" notes scribbled on the margins of yesterday's *Plain Dealer* and hastily left on the kitchen counter. The art of writing poetry can take time—even a lifetime—to perfect. Here, you'll get a day of poetry together, but you may want to make it a regular habit. You'll concoct full-fledged, mushy, inspired verse, penned in cursive on textured, softly hued paper.

Step by Step

10 A.M.: Begin your adventure in poetry by picking up the necessary supplies. The Writing Room is stocked with everything you'll need: stationery, specialized paper products, even books that can help get you started.

Yes, it sounds silly, but paper is important. If it weren't, you'd print your resume on the back of a paper bag and send it to a prospective employer in a recycled inter-office mail envelope. The weight of a piece of paper, its texture and hue, help create an aura of permanence in the mind of the recipient. Envelopes are important, too. Instead of a thin strip of glue, letters of long ago bore a bold wax seal— the author's personalized monogram or crest. Such seals, still available at specialty stores like the Writing Room, add a sense of commitment and even intrigue to your communiqué.

Smple pieces of slate, available all along the shores of Lake Erie, can have as lasting an effect as Moses's Ten Commandments.

Ribbon-wrapped scrolls serve well for an old-fashioned touch, and sometimes simple pieces of slate, available all along the shores of Lake Erie, can have as lasting an effect as Moses' Ten Commandments had on the Israelites. Be innovative with the mode of communication. Your words should be a lasting treasure, something your grandchild might find on the eve of her own wedding and call a good omen.

2 P.M.: Since the Eastman Reading Garden reopened with its bevy of reading gnomes, it has become an enchanted inner-city hangout for bookworms and writers alike. Located between the old Cleveland Public Library building and the new library annex, it is the perfect spot to spend a quiet morning reading or writing—and if you find yourself stuck on a line or a rhyme scheme, the reference section is in the building just next door. While away the hours on a bench here, bouncing ideas off each other, and writing lines as they come to you, creating poetry together that is all of your own making. Write your lines and verses without a care for how silly they may sound, writing and editing until both of you are satisfied with your poems.

8 P.M. (or when there's a poetry reading scheduled near you): Share your

poem in public. The poetry scene in Cleveland's cafes and bars has expanded recently due in part to the popularity of poetry slams (competitions in which local poets write and recite poems on the spur of the moment in front of live crowds). Poets young and old can be found at these events. With your own poem in hand, go out to hear some live poetry. Perhaps you'll have the guts to get up and read it out loud, proclaiming your love to all the muses of Cleveland.

Variation:

THE ONE-DAY EPIC POEM: For some, a single poem is not enough. A "miniseries" twist can add merriment to the game. Leave the first stanza by her coffee cup in the morning; the second stanza, slip into her briefcase; have the third delivered to the office along with a formal invitation to dinner; put the fourth under her plate at the restaurant. The fifth? Well, you can deliver the fifth stanza in any number of creative ways.

However you deliver your message, know that this type of romantic wordplay is the surefire way to woo as lovers do.

Directory

Cleveland Public Library
325 Superior Ave., Cleveland
216-623-2800
HOURS/AVAILABILITY:
Mon-Sat 9 a.m.–6 p.m.,
Sun 1 p.m.–5 p.m.

Poets' League of Greater Cleveland
2304 N. St. James Parkway, Cleveland
216-932-8444
HOURS/AVAILABILITY:
Call for monthly poetry schedules.

Writing Room
28699 Chagrin Blvd., Woodmere Village
216-831-9717
HOURS/AVAILABILITY:
Mon–Wed, Fri, and Sat
10 a.m.–6 p.m.,
Thu 10 a.m.–7 p.m.

Outing 5
SWING!

Season: Any ~ **Time:** 10 hours (with a 2-hour break)
Location: Near West/Downtown
Intimacy level: 1–2 ~ **Cost:** $$$–$$$$
Advance planning: none

What You'll Do

🕊 Shop in the underground world of vintage clothing ($15–$80).

🕊 Go home to spruce up and get ready for the evening.

🕊 Dine in Cleveland's past ($50–$100).

🕊 Dance and swing through the Warehouse District ($30–$50).

🕊 Wind down with a nightcap ($15–$40).

NOTE: *Choose a Wednesday or Thursday night for swing dancing. If a one-day shopping blitz isn't quite your style, spread these activities out over a week or so—especially if you're squeamish about wearing off-the-rack clothes before washing and pressing them first. Here, we've jam-packed a day with events for reference.*

There is something so enticing about the World War II era. The clothes, the music, the style. It's no surprise that every 10 years or so swing dancing finds its way to yet another generation of dancers—maybe it never really leaves.

When I was young, my brother managed a show called *Stompin' at the State,* modeled after '30s- and '40s-style live radio shows broadcast from the State Theater downtown. People would dress up and go to the then-run-down State Theater for an evening of dancing, food, and fun. I'll never forget my education in swing at the State Theater.

Spiffing up in '40s-style clothes, learning the jitterbug with your partner, and dancing to big band sounds makes for a night of pure romantic exuberance. Learning—and pulling off—complicated dance steps requires teamwork and togetherness. While learning these steps well you can develop your style as a couple. Frolicking to the optimistic sounds of swing and listening to old torch songs can really get you "In the Mood."

Step by Step

2 P.M.: Shop for vintage goodies. The Cleveland Shop has an upscale collection of clothing and jewelry from the 1920s to the 1970s. Just across the street, Chelsea's is a veritable warehouse of couture, arranged in a pleasingly organized fashion. More than 8,000 square feet of space in this store are devoted to clothing organized by era, style, and color. "The swing era is becoming really popular," says owner Nancy Wilson. "Girls come in to find a dress that they can dance in—a dress that moves."

Shopping in these places is like wandering into grandma's attic. You'll find treasures and enjoy the simple pleasures of playing dress-up as if you were rummaging through an old forgotten trunk.

5:15 P.M.: Pick up your bags and head home to don your new dancing clothes and get dolled up for an evening on the town.

7 P.M.: Enjoy a quiet, candlelit dinner at your next stop, Traci's Restaurant in Ohio City. Though small in size, Traci's is big on atmosphere. This

Develop your style as a couple.
Frolicking to the optimistic sounds of swing
and listening to old torch songs
can really get you "in the Mood."

otherwise nondescript building makes its mark on the surrounding Ohio City neighborhood with a small cupola that sits atop the building, lending an almost nautical look to the edifice.

Underneath Traci's mini-tower you'll find cuisine from every region of Italy. Jim Traci, whose family has occupied this corner of Ohio City since 1939, calls the cuisine "upscale, home-style Italian." The sauces, entrees, and wines that are served at the cozy tables here represent an eclectic mix of Italian fare. Most evenings you can warm up to the sounds of a live pianist as you sip on a cocktail or peruse the wine list. The music is a fabulous aperitif to complement the hearty entree of big band sounds yet to come. You'll be tempted to lounge, recline, and order every dish on the menu. Resist the temptation. Explain to your waiter that you have an evening of dancing planned, and ask for a meal that is high in carbs and light on the sauces and meats.

8:30 P.M.: Burn off those calories by dancing at Spy. Every Wednesday and Thursday night is Swing Night at Spy. At this trendy spot, high ceilings are flanked with hand-crafted wood treatments, carefully planned lighting adds atmosphere, and velvet furniture and draperies bring an almost indescribable allure to the room.

The dance floor at Spy comes alive with a hopping throng of young and old, and those interested in learning such classic steps as the jitterbug, or even the Charleston, can arrive at 8 to take lessons before the real dancing starts.

In addition to the dance floor, the thoughtfully appointed Spy is filled with little nooks in which to hide away from the throng in plush chairs and couches while sipping on a cosmopolitan. A fireplace and bookshelves turn one area of the club into a sort of library, while heavy velvet curtains conceal guests in yet another nook. The atmosphere at Spy is perfect for this dress-up night—elegant but fun.

1 A.M.: Just down the street is a favorite late-night stop, the Liquid Café. Large velvet couches set just in front of the floor-to-ceiling windows invite you to kick back with a glass of brandy and enjoy the view of the city from the Warehouse District. From this vantage-point, you can see the top of the Terminal Tower and watch other late-night stragglers strolling on W. 6th St.

You may, after just one evening like this, find yourself addicted to the foofy clothes and snappin' rhythms of yesteryear. Fear not, Cleveland's underground swing scene has been around for a long time, and it isn't going anywhere.

Variations:

If you're really serious about learning all the right moves, take a class together. There is no shortage of dance classes in the area, and you'll receive personalized attention from a professional instructor. Cavana Dance on the east and south sides of town is just one of the places around town where you can take classes for one evening or up to six weeks. Or, call your neighborhood's community center to see if they offer swing dancing classes. Since schedules and times vary throughout the year, call ahead and reserve your space.

Directory

Cavana Ball Room
4189 Pearl Rd., Parma
216-398-7660
HOURS/AVAILABILITY:
Class schedule varies.

Cavana Dance Studio
19032 Detroit Rd, Rocky River
440-333-1585
HOURS/AVAILABILITY:
Class schedule varies.

Chelsea's
1412 W. 116th St., Cleveland
216-226-9147
HOURS/AVAILABILITY:
Tue–Sat 11 a.m.–6 p.m.

Cleveland Shop
11606 Detroit Ave., Cleveland
216-228-9725
HOURS/AVAILABILITY:
Open 6 days a week; hours
are seasonal; please call.

Liquid Café
1212 W. 6th St., Cleveland
216-479-7717
HOURS/AVAILABILITY:
Daily 4:30 p.m.–2:30 a.m.

Spy
1261 W. 6th St., Cleveland
216-621-7907
HOURS/AVAILABILITY:
Swing dancing:
Thu 8 p.m.–2:30 a.m.
(lessons at 7 p.m.).

Traci's
2800 Clinton Ave., Cleveland
216-771-4744
HOURS/AVAILABILITY:
Mon–Thu 11:30 a.m.–
9:30 p.m., Fri 11:30 a.m.–
11 p.m., Sat 4:30 p.m.–
11 p.m., Sun closed

Outing 6
THE SUNSET

Season: Spring, Summer, Fall
Time: 3 hours ~ **Location:** West
Intimacy level: 1 ~ **Cost:** $
Advance planning: None

What You'll Do

- Drive—or rollerblade—to the banks of Lake Erie ($10 for overnight rollerblade rental).
- View a spectacular sunset.

  NOTE: *this itinerary assumes you're viewing a June sunset, when the sun sets at around 9 p.m. Check* The Plain Dealer *for daily sunset times.*

They happen almost every evening, so sunsets are perfect for the impulsive. Though the setting sun can be observed from almost anywhere in town, the best spots to witness the sun sinking on the western horizon are to be found along Cleveland's western shoreline. This simple pleasure is absolutely free and requires little more than a healthy set of eyes, and the romance of a single, fiery-red sunset can burn into your memory for years to come. A sunset is a colorful excuse for a first kiss or a long hug. It's a beautiful setting in which to present an engagement ring or a well-worded compliment. Or it's simply a great moment to be silent together.

Step by Step

6:30 P.M.: Rent rollerblades at the Wilderness Shop. Park your car at Rocky River Park (you might not want to skate back to the car through hazardous traffic at dusk) and take a skate before the sun's evening performance begins. Lake Avenue's stretch of flat pavement is a nice setting for a roll—or a stroll, if you're not on skates.

The pebble-covered shore is among the best places in Cleveland for the popular sport of stone skipping.

7:30 P.M.: Roll back over to Rocky River Park and drop off the skates at the car. This often-overlooked park has everything: a playground, good parking, a spot right on the beach, and a high cliff that offers an excellent view of the Western skyline. The pebble-covered shore is among the best places in Cleveland for the popular sport of stone skipping. Stone skippers dot the shoreline, counting out loud, "One, two, THREE . . . FOUR!" Others comb the area for multicolored pebbles appropriate for filling decorative jars at home.

For the best view of the sunset, walk up the steps to the cliff jutting out from the upper end of the park. From this perch, you'll have a bird's-eye view of the coming sunset, as sailboats glide over the twinkling sheen of the twilight lake on their way to and from the nearby Cleveland Yacht Club.

8:30 P.M.: Settle in to watch the sunset. Great sunsets are difficult to plan for, but there are a few factors that can add to the beauty of a sunset. Peter Whiting, Associate Professor of Geological Sciences at Case Western Reserve University, notes, "If the sun is shining in the afternoon, and you've had a rain, the sunset will be yellow to orange. If you've had no rain, dust particles are more likely to be scattered around the atmosphere, creating a sunset that is orange to red." Distant volcanic eruptions have an effect on the hue of our sunsets—even eruptions as far away as the Philippines, says Whiting.

Many couples have sunset rituals. Some place bets on exactly which minute the last bit of sun will sink below the horizon. Others will name every color they see. Still others simply hold hands and kiss when the evening's solar performance is finished. Develop your own ritual for watching the setting sun.

Whatever your approach to the sunset, you'll be moved by a stunning view in a charming part of the city. You might even choose to stay a spell after the sun sets, to see what kind of stargazing you can accomplish.

Variations

THE SUN ALSO SETS…IN MENTOR: One mile of beachfront property makes Mentor Headlands the longest beach in the state. Because of the extensive reach of this idyllic setting, it's easy to pretend that you're in an exotic South Pacific paradise. Plan a long walk along the shoreline, and be sure to take off your shoes to truly enjoy the sand and water between your toes. Pick an appropriate piece of driftwood to perch on, or bring along a thick blanket on which to rest while watching a beautiful sunset.

MILESTONE SUNSETS: If you're the type who keeps an eye on the calendar, then make two important appointments. Be sure to view the sunset on June 21, the summer solstice and the longest day of the year, logging in at 15 hours and 1 minute from sunrise to sunset. This is the very best use of a vacation day because it seems like there's a bit more in the bargain. At the end of the day, watch the sun go down. Stand on your tiptoes as the very last inch of the sphere disappears over the waters of Lake Erie. Also mark your calendar for December 21. Bundle up, and make your way back to your favorite spot—but much earlier in the day, as there are a mere 9 hours and 19 minutes

Typically, you'll want to stand with your back to the sun in order to catch a rainbow.
Whether you see a rainbow or not depends on where you are respective to the light.

of sunlight on this day. Take a moment to huddle together and congratulate yourselves—you've made it through the darkest portion of winter.

Catch a Rainbow

There's good news about the amount of precipitation we get here: we get to see rainbows. My cousin describes seeing a rainbow after having a romantic dinner with her then-boyfriend, Mike. "We were driving west over the Main Avenue Bridge, and all of a sudden there was a rainbow in the sky, arching perfectly over the bridge." She adds, with playful sarcasm, and just a smidgen of overacting, "that was the night I knew I loved Mike." Now she chases rainbows in her backyard with her husband and three bubbly toddlers.

Rainbows are elusive but awe-inspiring. Though there is no way to accurately predict where and when a rainbow will appear, you can increase your chances of finding one if you know when to look. "Rainbows are the result of light being scattered by raindrops, creating a prism effect as in a spectrum of colors," says Dr. Peter Whiting of Case Western Reserve University. So you are more likely to see rainbows in the spring and fall—when Northeast Ohio typically has more rainfall—and during the late afternoon to early evening hours, when precipitation is most likely.

"I guess if you saw a triple rainbow, you'd pretty much have to marry whomever you were standing next to at the time."

Typically, advises Whiting, you'll want to stand with your back to the sun in order to catch a rainbow. "Whether you see a rainbow or not depends on where you are respective to the light. Not everyone will see the rainbow, because the arch is consistent with the scattering of light in the atmosphere." Whiting claims to have seen double rainbows and warns that triple rainbows are dangerous. "I guess if you saw a triple rainbow, you'd pretty much have to marry whomever you were standing next to at the time."

Rainbow chasers who fail to find what they're looking for in the skies can settle for a garden-hose rainbow. Following Whiting's guidelines, stand with your back to the sun, and employ the mist function on your garden hose. Play with the angle of the mist until—there it is—a small rainbow appears.

If you find yourself in need of a rainbow in the off-season, you still have one last hope. Gloomy days can be revived with a creative arrangement of fruit. Following the color spectrum we all learned in grade school, ROY G BIV (red, orange, yellow, green, blue, indigo, violet), prepare a fruit salad made with watermelon, strawberries, or raspberries (red); oranges, mangos, or peaches (orange); starfruit (yellow); kiwi (green); blueberries (blue); blackberries or purple grapes (indigo—you'll have to cheat a little); and plums (violet).

Rose Griffith, who is among my local culinary heroes and holds a degree in food anthropology, has very strong opinions about victuals. When I asked her about this fruit rainbow of mine, her brow furrowed a bit. I knew I'd asked her a frivolous food question and quickly tried to change the subject.

But a while later the phone rang, and Rose had this to say: "You have to include mangos. Mangos are the most sensual fruit I know. You have to trust someone to eat mangos with him. It makes you vulnerable—juice running down your chin as you sink your teeth into its succulent flesh," she pauses, takes a deep breath. "Feed one another. Close your eyes and pretend you can feel the tropical breezes enveloping you. You might even see a rainbow forming above the waterfalls."

In the space of a moment, Griffith transformed this silly rainbow into a passionate interlude. Rose's husband is one lucky guy.

Directory

Mentor Headlands Beach State Park

9601 Headlands Rd., Mentor

440-352-8082

HOURS/AVAILABILITY:
Open daily 8 a.m.–sunset. Check sunset time in daily *Plain Dealer*.

Rocky River Park

20250 Beachcliff Blvd., Rocky River

440-331-0600 (City Hall)

HOURS/AVAILABILITY:
Check sunset time in daily *Plain Dealer*.

Wilderness Shop

18636 Detroit Rd., Lakewood

216-521-9100

HOURS/AVAILABILITY:
Mon 11 a.m.–9 p.m.,
Tue–Fri 10 a.m.–9 p.m.,
Sat 10 a.m.–6 p.m.,
Sun noon–5 p.m.

Outing 7

CLEVELAND'S ROMANTIC ARCHES

Seasons: All ~ **Time:** 4 hours
Location: Downtown ~ **Intimacy level:** 1
Cost: $$–$$$
Advance planning: None

What You'll Do

⏵ Take an informative walk through downtown's beautiful buildings.

⏵ Lunch in the historic Warehouse District ($35–$50).

⏵ Set out on a tour of the bridges in the Flats.

The curvaceous, sexy arch is the basis—both literally and metaphorically—of architecture. Cleveland is a city full of arches. Cleveland's bridges sport lengthy arches, while its buildings rely on dramatic, massive arches for support. Wonderful things happen under these arches each day. Stand directly under the arch of the Keybank building on the corner of Ontario and Rockwell, and you'll feel the presence of a thousand chance meetings, the great dreams of the men and women who built these lasting structures. You can walk through the city every day and not fully appreciate the significance lurking behind its walls. Take a day to really explore the city with the one you love, and discover a side of Cleveland you never quite saw before.

Step by Step

10 A.M.: Arrive at Tower City by car or RTA. The large arches at the front of Tower City's entryway are Cleveland's grandest, and walking through these gigantic doors onto Public Square is spectacular. The Terminal Tower is the defining structure of Cleveland's skyline and was, for years, the tallest building between New York and Chicago. A visionary creation, the Terminal Tower was built by the Van Sweringen brothers with the idea of connecting—via trains and light rails—the suburbs with downtown.

Next, make your way through the sites on Public Square, passing the Moses Cleaveland statue, the Soldiers and Sailors Monument, and the lamp sculpture at the Society for Savings building. Though small, this is quite a significant lamp, as it represents the first successful use of electric streetlights in the world, sparking the burgeoning electric industry in Cleveland—and in the world—in 1879. The Society bank building, on which that famous lamp is hinged, is supported by large archways that lead into one of the city's grandest bank lobbies.

Walk east, toward East 9th and Superior Avenue. St. John's Cathedral marks the beginning of the Civic Center area with its gothic arches.

NOON: Head north on East 9th Street and walk toward Lakeside Avenue, where the expansive Mall areas stretch out to the lake. The Fountain of Eternal Life borders the West Mall area at St. Clair between Ontario and East 6th. Northward, city hall (at Lakeside Avenue, just West of East 6th) houses Archibald Willard's famous *Spirit of '76* painting.

It used to be a dangerous, scary place reminiscent of a film noir set. In the old days, only the truly tough went to the "Industrial Flats."

Now you're ready for lunch. Walk west on Lakeside to West 6th Street. The Bradley Building was among the first historic sites in the district to be remodeled for residential use. At the corner of West 6th and St. Clair, the Hoyt Block, dedicated in 1876, houses the Blue Point Grille. The Blue Point features a dramatic interior accented by high ceilings, intricate woodwork—both restored and new—and floor-to-ceiling windows that look out on the vibrant Warehouse District. Request a window seat and enjoy munching on marlin or swordfish steaks while taking in the spectacular view of the Warehouse District and Public Square.

1 P.M.: Curve through the Flats. If you have lived in Cleveland less than 10 years, you probably know the Flats as simply an entertainment center. However, it used to be a dangerous, scary place reminiscent of a *film noir* set. The most interesting eatery was "the old Fagan's," modeled after one-room country pubs in Ireland. In the old days, only the truly tough went to the "Industrial Flats," as it was then called. Poet Allen Ginsberg was so affected by the area, he wrote a poem called "Cleveland, the Flats" in which he describes driving through the abandoned streets. It's a jagged, beautiful poem: "Smoking organpipes of God in the Cleveland Flats." By the end of the poem he is making an escape, it seems, to University Circle, chanting a protective mantra to himself.

The smokestacks, bridges, and warehouses that made up this formerly industrial part of the city are still there. Take a moment and look past the neon lights and Johnny-come-lately watering holes to peer at the lasting treasures of the Industrial Revolution. Thirteen operational bridges and two historic bridges ("historic" meaning they no longer work, but sure add nicely to the landscape) make up the unusual architecture of the Flats.

These and other noteworthy structures are pointed out on a tour of the Flats provided by the Flats Oxbow Association. This tour is well worth the time and effort, for here you'll discover a Cleveland you never knew. The site where Moses Cleaveland landed is commemorated on the east bank of the Flats, as is the Lorenzo and Rebecca Carter Cabin, at Heritage Park. Other notable sites in the Flats include the Powerhouse with its unmistakable smokestacks and the underbelly of the Detroit-Superior Bridge—Cleveland's first high-level bridge to span the Cuyahoga. These are some of the structures that in the 1920s and 1930s inspired photographer Margaret Bourke-White to take striking pictures immortalizing Cleveland as a productive center of industry.

3 P.M.: Finish the afternoon at the Watermark with a snack on the riverside patio. The building has served a variety of purposes in the history of the Flats, providing a work place for Portuguese fishermen, industrial suppliers, and even rubber workers. A boat restorationist who occupied the building rescued the old dinghy that now hangs above the bar at the Watermark. The Watermark was among the very first restoration projects that helped to spur growth in the Flats. Owner Hap Gray took a great leap of faith when opening an upscale restaurant in what was considered, in the 1970s and 1980s, a "wasteland." "People laughed at us," says Gray. They're not laughing now. The Watermark has continued to improve the facility, adding a second level of outdoor patio seating, along with a glassed-in upper-deck patio for winter visitors.

Watermark makes its mark with fresh seafood specialties and also serves a tasty plate of eggs Benedict for Sunday brunch. From the riverside patio, you can study this stunning view and see first hand the interplay of the large freighters (my favorite is the Medusa Cement rig) and small boats. If you time your day properly, you can catch the brilliant show of color as the evening sun says goodnight to the Cuyahoga River and Lake Erie.

Variations

WHEN SHOE LEATHER WEARS THIN: Trolley Tours of Cleveland offers one- and two-hour tours daily highlighting some of Cleveland's most interesting neighborhoods and providing a noteworthy overview of the city and its great history. Trolley tours are reliable, and the tour guides are friendly. The trolley also provides shelter on cold, rainy, or unpredictably stormy days.

Directory

Blue Point Grille
700 West St. Clair Ave, Cleveland
216-875-7827
HOURS/AVAILABILITY:
Mon–Thu 11:30 a.m.–3 p.m.
and 5 p.m.–10:30 p.m.,
Fri 11:30 a.m.–3 p.m.
and 4 p.m.–11:30 p.m.,
Sat 4 p.m.–11:30 p.m.,
Sun 4 p.m.–9 p.m.

Flats Oxbow Association
1283 Riverbed St., Cleveland
216-566-1046
HOURS/AVAILABILITY:
Mon–Fri 8:30 a.m.–5 p.m.

Trolley Tours of Cleveland
216-771-4484
HOURS/AVAILABILITY:
Times vary, call for reservation.

Watermark Restaurant
1250 Old River Rd., Cleveland
216-241-1600
HOURS/AVAILABILITY:
Mon–Thu 11:30 a.m.–
10:00 p.m., Fri–
Sat 11:30 a.m.–11 p.m.,
Sun 10 a.m.–2:30 p.m.
(brunch) and 5 p.m.–10 p.m.

Outing 8

DON'T SEND FLOWERS– GO TO THEM

Season: Winter ~ **Time:** 4 hours
Location: East ~ **Intimacy level:** 1
Cost: $$–$$$
Advance planning: None

What You'll Do

🌸 Immerse yourself in flowers and spring air at the Rockefeller Greenhouse in University Circle.

🌸 Have lunch in a splash of color and spice at Sergio's ($35–$50).

🌸 Forage for flowers to take home from a nearby favorite flower shop ($10–$30).

The first few months of the year in Cleveland can bring us down. Venerable local weatherman Dick Goddard spends the first quarter of each year predicting not only cold, but clouds, clouds, clouds. He estimates that in the month of January, Northeast Ohioans will be treated to a sunny day only 30 percent of the time.

These are months when it's easy to lose sight of romance. Perhaps Valentine's Day is placed in February to remind all of us that one can find love even in the throes of winter. Even in Cleveland. These months of slush and gray sky were made for hibernation, cuddling, and cozying up by a fire; but even that can get repetitive and dull after a while. Maybe it's time to cheat winter—just for a day.

Step by Step

10 A.M.: You needn't fly to Florida to find a sultry slice of paradise. At University Circle, you'll find yourself in a world transformed from gray to colorful, dry and cold to balmy. At the Rockefeller Park Greenhouse you'll step straight into springtime.

When you first walk into this greenhouse, you'll notice the flowers, of course, as well as the hand-laid cobblestones and bricks and the carved stone fountain. But what will truly take your breath away is the humidity! That balmy nuisance you'll curse come the 4th of July is now, in the winter, a welcome friend that surrounds you with unseasonable kindness and warmth. Take off your coat and stay a while. You may decide to return to the greenhouse each week during winter, just to rehydrate.

Once you've acclimated, stroll through the greenhouse. The trick to really enjoying this adventure, especially in winter, is pretending. Let yourself think that it's a bright summer afternoon, and take your time meandering through the hundreds of varieties of flora to be found at this tucked-away treasure. Dress in bright layers to come to the greenhouse, and as your body temperature readjusts, peel off a layer or two just for fun. Come armed with a nose for unseasonable smells and an eye for welcome color.

Each January, the greenhouse hosts a late winter flower display when winter plants and flowers start to bloom. What a fantastic sight for sore eyes! Flowers in bloom all around you as you stroll, arm in

The orchid room, with its delicate climate,
offers visitors a lesson in fragility.
If you time your visit right,
the lilies may even be taking over the orchids.

arm, through the warm greenhouse while cold winds rage outside—you'll feel like you've outsmarted Old Man Winter.

The palm house is home to such species as the grapefruit tree, ponderosa lemon, fruit orange, and banana tree. Farther down the path, caffeine lovers can pay homage to the resident coffee tree. The orchid room, with its delicate climate, offers visitors a lesson in fragility. If you time your visit right, the lilies may even be taking over the orchids. Breathe deeply; you won't catch a scent like this outside of the greenhouse for a while.

NOON: You should have worked up an appetite by now. Make your way up Martin Luther King Boulevard to colorful, festive Sergio's.

Owners Sergio and Susan Abramof designed the layout and color scheme of the restaurant with summer in mind. Large, tropical palm trees stretch the full 15 feet to the ceilings, passing by walls of deep-sea blue and bright primary red. The food here is "a cross-cultural menu with a Brazilian twist," says Sergio. The smells wafting through this magical place conjure up an atmosphere full of spice and excess, creating the illusion of a seaside resort in Rio.

Brazilian born, Abramof chose the warm colors and palm trees in the dining room to enhance the Brazilian experience for his customers. But he admits the atmosphere allows him to think that maybe he's not really in Cleveland during these hard months.

Let the exotic aromas at Sergio's throw you into an equatorial frenzy the moment you enter. Indulge in every course—lingering over the spicy special soups of the day—and ask your waiter to suggest fruity wine, robust, colorful entrees, and a decadent dessert. Take your time eating as if it were a lazy summer afternoon, and pretend you really are at that resort in Rio.

1:30 P.M.: Don't let your day end quite yet. If it's truly gloomy out, stop on the way home for some fresh flowers. Cleveland is a funny place for flowers. It's one of the ironic things about the city—here we are in a part of the world that has so few sunny days, and yet we have hardly any open flower markets. Cleveland retailers could take a lesson from those in rainy Seattle, where it's a rare city block that isn't overrun on at least one corner with flowers screaming to be purchased.

Our local solution for this outing is Brunswick Florist. The funky facade of Brunswick is reminiscent of the 1950s. The florist's location on the campus of the Cleveland Clinic Foundation means high volume, so you'll have plenty of fresh flowers from which to choose. Make up a bouquet for yourself that is bursting with color and aroma.

To finish off your day, stick those flowers in a vase and place them directly next to a bathtub filled with bubbles—or set them on your night table and let the aroma scent your dreams during a mid-winter siesta.

Variations

IN A TROPICAL JUNGLE: Cleveland's other indoor gem in the wintertime is the Cleveland Metroparks RainForest. The climate in this self-contained environment is kept at a temperature and humidity level consistent with a tropical rain forest—complete with a thunderstorm every few minutes. As you walk through this tropical paradise, birds soar overhead while anteaters search for lunch, and bats twitch and whoosh.

After your jungle adventure, stop at Johnny's for a late lunch or early dinner in a cozy Mediterranean climate. Among the most touted restaurants in town, Johnny's serves fresh Italian food according to family recipes used for generations.

Directory

Brunswick Florist
10550 Carnegie Ave., Cleveland
216-421-4800

HOURS/AVAILABILITY:
Mon–Fri 8:30 a.m.–5:30 p.m.,
Sat 9 a.m.–5 p.m., Sun closed

Cleveland Metroparks Zoo and The RainForest
3900 Wildlife Way, Cleveland
216-661-6500

HOURS/AVAILABILITY:
Daily 10 a.m.–5 p.m. (the RainForest is open Wed until 9 p.m.); extended Summer weekend and holiday hours, please call.

Johnny's on Fulton
3164 Fulton Rd., Cleveland
216-281-0055

HOURS/AVAILABILITY:
Mon–Thu 11:30 a.m.–
3 p.m. and 5 p.m.–10 p.m.,
Fri 11:30 a.m.–3 p.m.
and 5 p.m.–11 p.m., Sat
5 p.m.–11 a.m., Sun closed

Rockefeller Park Greenhouse
750 E. 88th St., Cleveland
216-664-3103

HOURS/AVAILABILITY:
Daily 10 a.m.–4 p.m.

Sergio's in University Circle
1903 Ford Drive, Cleveland
216-231-1234

HOURS/AVAILABILITY:
Mon–Thu 11:30 a.m.–
2:30 p.m. and
5:30 p.m.–9:30 p.m.,
Fri 11:30 a.m.–2:30 p.m.
and 5:30 p.m.–11 p.m.,
Sat 5:30 p.m.–11 p.m. Reservations recommended.

Outing 9

THE TRAPPINGS OF LOVE

Season: All ~ **Time:** 4 hours
Location: West ~ **Intimacy level:** 2–3
Cost: $$
Advance planning: None

What You'll Do

- Shop together for milestone gifts at specialty stores; develop wish lists together for the coming year.
- Reward yourselves with a shopper's late lunch ($25–$40).

*Y*ou're stuck. Again. What to get her? This question has stumped many a great man in the past, and can be counted among the true struggles of a romantic relationship. To be certain that you're on the right track, try out a revolutionary idea: shop together. Couples rack their brains over what to get each other for birthdays and holidays, playing a dangerous game of ESP. Shopping together is the only way to really know what the other person wants, and if you plan properly you can pack a year's worth of shopping into one day, solidifying another year together in one romantic afternoon.

Don't make the mistakes of the romantically challenged. Plan ahead, be thoughtful, and be inventive when giving a gift to your sweetheart. Take note of the catalogues he or she likes. When you hear the phrase, "I wish I had . . ." pay close attention to what follows. And once or twice a year, take the time to shop together. Pick a few stores that carry an array of things both of you like, develop a relationship with the shop owners and clerks, and make a practice of returning throughout the year to purchase items from your love's wish list.

Step by Step

2 P.M.: Visit Rocky River's "Olde Tudor Row" on Lake Avenue in Rocky River, and begin at Tracy & Co. This is an eclectic store that carries household items, antiques, and works by local artisans and provides such services as framing and home decorating. Shopping here is a pleasure as Tracy and her mother flit about the store making suggestions to customers, saying hello to friends who stop in, and arranging new displays. Take with you a pen and a pad of paper, making note of items you like. Tracy will keep a wish list for you in her card file. In the space of an afternoon, you've accomplished your shopping goals for the year. The big event for men at Tracy & Co. is Cigar Night, which happens every year a few weeks before Christmas. Men are invited into the store for cognac and fine stogies while they shop at a discount. "It's great fun," says owner Tracy Sheahan. "The guys come in and do all their shopping in one night, and then they're done."

Once you've created your list at Tracy & Co., take a walk through the neighborhood, discovering shops along the way. The Avalon Gallery houses paintings, prints, and pottery representing a wide range of styles from a host of local and national artists. For a truly special creation, visit Visage Portrait Design. Here you can look through various styles of photographic portraits by Julie Walborn and schedule an appointment to have your portrait taken as a couple. The sitting fee (which is around $55) can include just the two of you, or you, the kids, and even grandma. The shop also maintains

The big event for men at Tracy & Co. is Cigar Night. Men are invited into the store for cognac and fine stogies while they shop at a discount.

connections with local artisans who create hand-crafted frames to suit even the most discriminating taste.

4 P.M.: Shopped out? Have a late shoppers' lunch at Danny Boy's, a pizza place with plenty of character. The house specialty is a Woogie Bear, a fold-over pizza served with extra sauce. Enjoy the atmosphere at Danny Boy's—a mixture of antiques, plenty of lacquered wood, and a smidgen of Italian flare—while you go over your gift wish list one last time for reinforcement.

Variations

EAST SIDE BOUTIQUE SHOPPING: For East Siders, the boutiques and shops at Shaker Square offer similar customer service. Mary Brown's Ohio Signatures is the place to find unusual women's clothes and accessories. Like Tracy & Co. on the West Side, Brown keeps customer wish lists, augmented by mailing campaigns and sales. "We have fiercely loyal customers," says Brown, adding, "some come from the West Coast once a year to shop here. Husbands know that we keep tabs on their wife's taste, and they feel comfortable shopping here because they know they're getting what their wives want."

Stroll through Shaker Square's shops and stop for some authentic Mexican food at Lucita's on the Square where the chimichangas will fill you, and the burritos are a textured mix of beans and grilled meat of your choice.

CAVING IN TO THE MALL: Admittedly, there are times when only a mall will do. One couple I know handles malls like this: They arrive on a slow shopping day—say a Monday afternoon—and set a time limit of one or two hours. Then they split up to shop, visiting the stores they like best and taking detailed notes on the items they want, noting each item, its price, and even the bar-code number. At the end of the two hours, they meet for a mall meal, exchange lists, and then shop for each other. Each receives some items that he or she wants, plus leaving the mall with a reliable, easy-to-follow list of "acceptable" future gifts. I think it's brilliant.

Directory

Avalon Gallery

20163 Lake Rd., Rocky River
440-331-3776

HOURS/AVAILABILITY:
Tue–Fri 11 a.m.–6 p.m.,
Sat noon–6 p.m., Sun–Mon
by appointment

Danny Boy's Italian Eatery

20251 Lake Rd., Rocky River
440-333-9595

HOURS/AVAILABILITY:
Mon–Thu 11 a.m.–10 p.m.,
Fri–Sat 11 a.m.–11 p.m.

Lucita's Mexican Restaurant

13112 Shaker Square,
Shaker Heights
216-561-8537

HOURS/AVAILABILITY:
Tue–Thu 11:30 a.m.–10 p.m.,
Fri 11:30 a.m.–11 p.m.,
Sat 5 p.m.–1 p.m.,
Sun 5 p.m.–9 p.m.

Ohio Signatures

3101 Shaker Square, Cleveland
216-561-5665

HOURS/AVAILABILITY:
Mon and Thu 10 a.m.–8 p.m.,
Tue–Sat 10 a.m.–6 p.m.,
Sun 1 p.m.– 5p.m.

Tracy & Co.

20117 Lake Rd., Rocky River
440-331-1613

HOURS/AVAILABILITY:
Tue–Sat 11 a.m.–6 p.m.,
Wed 11 a.m.–8 p.m.

Visage Portrait Design

20141 Lake Ave., Rocky River
440-333-6268

HOURS/AVAILABILITY:
Photos by appointment only.

Outing 10
YOU RUB MY BACK...

Season: Any ~ **Time:** 3 hours
Location: Southeast
Intimacy level: 2–3 ~ **Cost:** $$
Advance Planning: Some

What You'll Do

- Learn the art of massage ($25–$50).
- Get a rubdown.

  NOTE: *You'll need to place a call to the Cleveland School of Massage to find out when the next couples massage class takes place and schedule a free massage with a student at the school immediately following your class.*

*I*ntimacy takes many forms, and one of the most popular is the indulgent massage. One year my cousin and her husband-to-be, both suffering from the "early-career bank-account blues," gave each other "gift certificates" for massages at Christmastime, redeemable on demand in the weeks following the holiday. It must have worked well for them—now they're married with three kids and can often be seen rubbing each other's shoulders between diaper changes and trips to the store for more milk. I say take a man to a massage, and he's relaxed for a day—teach him to give a massage, and *you're* relaxed for a lifetime! Though we all know the basics of massage, the experience can only be enhanced with education. So warm up those hands, and prepare to learn—together—the art of massage.

Step by Step

7 P.M.: Take a couples massage class. At these classes, novices can learn—together—the basics of the art of massage, in classes that teach both relaxing and stimulating massage techniques.

8 P.M.: After the class, get a massage from a trained professional—or a professional-in-training. In order to earn credits toward their degree and accreditation, students at the school give free massages. Why not help them out a bit? You get a massage, the student gets his certificate, everyone's happy. Of course, a tip is encouraged, and an instructor is always on hand to oversee the student's work.

Variations:

UPSCALE APPROACH: The Denise Alexander salon offers comprehensive packages that include skin care, massotherapy, facials, pedicures, and manicures. "It's soothing to the spirit, a personal escape, and a wonderful gift to give to others," says proprietor Denise Alexander, who operates a calming, European-style salon, equipped with the most modern furniture and mini-spa rooms—you'll feel like Captain Kirk on the bridge of the *Enterprise* when you're sitting in the pedicure room. The lighting is low, relaxing you the moment you walk through the front door. The staff is very professional and accommodating and can handle a facial, a Swedish massage, or a relaxing pedicure with ease and grace. Going together ensures you're simpatico in mood upon completion of your self-indulgent relaxation.

Taking time out to relax and indulge can soothe spirits—and tempers, if need be. Spend a day together devoted to relaxation, and

I say take a man to a massage,
and he's relaxed for a day.
Teach him to give a massage,
and you're relaxed for a lifetime.

take note of the effects on your week. And later, when you're practicing your massotherapy techniques on each other, for heaven's sake, go that extra five minutes. It makes all the difference in the world.

REDUCING DAILY STRESS: Is your loved one stressed out at work? Kidnap him or her for a quick rubdown at lunchtime at the Cleveland Athletic Club, which has an on-staff masseuse who can provide a quick escape from stress (you don't have to be a member of the Athletic Club to get a massage).

Directory

Cleveland Athletic Club
1118 Euclid Ave., Cleveland
216-621-8900
HOURS/AVAILABILITY:
Call for appointment. (Massages are available
to non-members.)

Cleveland School of Massage
10683 Ravenna Rd., Twinsburg
330-405-1933
HOURS/AVAILABILITY:
Call for class times.

Denise Alexander
19275 Detroit Rd., Rocky River
440-333-9991
HOURS/AVAILABILITY:
Call for appointment
(closed Sun–Mon).

Outing 11
RIDING THE WAVES OF LAKE ERIE

Season: Spring, Summer, Fall
Time: 6 hours ~ **Location:** Downtown/West
Intimacy level: 2 ~ **Cost:** $–$$$$
Advance Planning: Some

What You'll Do

- Ride the afternoon waves on Lake Erie.
- Take a cool dip.
- Dine in a Cleveland sailor's landmark.

NOTE: *You'll have to call ahead to charter a boat or jet skis, and, of course, check the weather the day you go.*

*R*iding the waves of Lake Erie is among the most romantic and exciting pastimes available in this area—if you leave it to the experts. The relatively shallow waters of Lake Erie combined with prevailing westerly winds make for a challenging ride, whether you're on a lightweight jet ski or a 40-foot yacht. On the lake you can escape the city and enter a realm where the only sounds you hear are made by waves lapping against the hull and an occasional seagull.

Step by Step

3 P.M.: Start your sail. On the high end, Sail and Charter can pick you up in a Bentley or a Rolls Royce and deliver you to *Res Ipsa Loquitur*, a

Columbia 50 yacht owned and operated by Larry Lanscover. This service will tool you around the lake with all the accoutrements for a price that really says, "I love you." (Around $1,000 for a four-hour trip.) The yacht is fitted with luxurious furniture and comes with a knowledgeable captain. All you need to do is sit back and enjoy the view. The cost may be prohibitive for all but the most special occasions, but the boat can comfortably accommodate up to 40—so it's not out of reach if you can get a few friends together to create a special evening on the waters at a cost of $50 per couple.

If togetherness—alone—is what you seek, and 50 feet is too much space for you, your love, and your wallet, less expensive alternatives are certainly available. Located in the Flats, Great Lakes Water Sports can outfit you with a rental boat or jet skis and all the fixin's for a great time on the lake. Keep in mind that traffic on the Cuyahoga River increases every year, and you should familiarize yourself with the laws of boating before you hit the waters (don't worry, you'll get a quick lesson before you leave the dock). And also be aware of the zero tolerance law upheld by the Coast Guard. Even one empty beer can on board, or on your person, can set you back immensely in fines and possible jail time.

4 P.M.: Plan a swim. Whether you're boating or jet skiing, make your way out to the lake from the Cuyahoga River and explore the shoreline. Traveling west, you'll soon run into Edgewater Park. The western half of the beach area is reserved for boaters and jet skiers and is designated as safe for dropping anchor and taking a swim. Relax in the water and enjoy the sunshine and the time spent floating together.

Lollygag your way along the west shoreline of the lake, exploring the shale cliffs or searching for landmarks. Legend has it that some of the crevices and holes in the shale cliffs once were actually tunnels used as final getaway points for travelers on the Underground Railroad. Later, those same tunnels would be used for illegally importing Canadian "hooch" during Prohibition.

6 P.M.: Plan a dockside dinner, but avoid the throngs of rowdy boaters at the Flats by setting your course instead for Sweetwater Landing at the Emerald Necklace Marina. To get there, pass Lakewood Park pier. Soon afterwards you'll see the Detroit Avenue Bridge spanning the Rocky River. The Cleveland Yacht Club marks the entrance to the river, and just upstream from the CYC is a dock and the round spire of the Sweetwater. Owned by Clevelander Gary Lucarelli, the Sweetwater is a nautical structure with an interesting menu of sandwiches, salads, and ice cream. The combined view of the Metroparks

and the river ensures that every seat in this round glass-enclosed restaurant is a good one. Enjoy your meal and prepare to head back to the Flats to return the boat.

Variations

LET SOMEONE ELSE DO THE WORK: Boating, especially in small craft, is not for everyone. The *Goodtime III* is large, and reminiscent of an era when passenger lines still traversed Lake Erie. This ship, flooded with romance, has been an institution in Cleveland since 1924, when the original *Goodtime* ferried passengers from Cleveland to Cedar Point and back. The Goodtime Cruise Line has been a family-run business since 1958, when the Fryan family christened the *Goodtime II*. In 1991, the family commissioned the *Goodtime III*—the largest day-passenger-excursion ship on the Great Lakes. On the *Goodtime III*, tours through the Flats and out on the lake are available throughout the day; these offer a slow-paced view of the bridges and trellises of the Flats and a lovely gander at the expansive Northeast Ohio shoreline as well as the waters stretching north toward Canada. Dinner-dance and moonlight cruises are available in the evenings.

Crevices and holes in the shale cliffs once were actually tunnels used as final getaway points for travelers on the Underground Railroad.

After your excursion, stop by Don's Lighthouse Grille. Built by an immigrant named Poschke who sold hot dogs from that spot in the 1920s, the Lighthouse is an institution along the West Shoreway. The building's four spiral towers are a landmark for sailors and weary Shoreway travelers alike. Inside, diners look out on Edgewater Park through giant arched windows while indulging in Don's fresh fish entrees. Die-hard Don's fans await the return of Don's Dirty Rice, a beefy concoction of rice, onions, and mushrooms that is still dearly missed years after its removal from the menu. Casual bar customers and weather-weary sailors might feel more comfortable stumbling into Don's pub area, where they can munch on mussels and hearty burgers and sip cold beers. The bar area is where fisherman chatter about "the one that got away" or yachtsmen tell tales of vast amounts of money spent on their hobby.

ON A SMALLER SCALE: There's a small-scale way to make a hobby of yachting. If you're so inclined, you need not travel farther than your own local hobby store to get find what you need. Say it with me five times fast: toy boat! Nowadays, these boats are engine-powered, and they are great way to while away the hours on a Saturday afternoon at the park, or for a Sunday evening in your very own tub. This pastime is as enjoyable today as it was a century ago and is a good way to incorporate the romance of sailing into a family setting.

Once you've built your boat, take it for a sail. Some of the better places for sailing toy boats include Wade Oval Pond in University Circle, Beyer's Pond in Strongsville, and Clague Park Pond in Westlake.

Directory

Don's Lighthouse Grille
8905 Lake Ave., Cleveland
216-961-6700

HOURS/AVAILABILITY:
Mon–Thu 11:30 a.m.–
2:30 p.m. and 5 p.m.–10 p.m.,
Fri 11:30 a.m.–2:30 p.m.
and 5 p.m.–11 p.m.,
Sat 5 p.m.–11 p.m.,
Sun 4:30 p.m.–9 p.m.

Goodtime III
216-861-5110

HOURS/AVAILABILITY:
Times vary, call for schedule.

Great Lakes Water Sports
1148 Main Ave., Cleveland
216-771-4386

HOURS/AVAILABILITY:
Times vary; call ahead
for reservations.

Sail and Charter
55 Public Square, Ste. 1040,
Cleveland
216-241-7007

HOURS/AVAILABILITY:
Call for appointment.

Sweetwater Landing
1500 Scenic Park Dr., Lakewood
216-228-2233

HOURS/AVAILABILITY:
April–November daily
10 a.m.–8:30 p.m.

Outing 12

A BERRY GOOD TIME...

Season: Spring, Summer, Fall
Time: 2–4 hours ~ **Location:** Southeast
Intimacy level: 1 ~ **Cost:** $
Advance planning: None

What You'll Do

- Pick your own seasonal fruit fresh from the vine ($10–$15).
- Wield a paring knife through your harvest in the afternoon sun.
- Make a sumptuously fruity dessert.

The climate and soil in Northeast Ohio are very friendly to fruit farmers and dairy producers. This is good news for peaches-and-cream enthusiasts who demand that only in-season fresh foods are served on their tables in the summer months. There is something very, well, Old Testament about picking fruit from the tree and offering it to your loved one. Biting into the flesh of a fresh peach and catching its juice with the back of your hand, then sharing a fruitful kiss is almost . . . sinful.

Practically every week of the summer and fall brings into season a different fruit or berry that awaits picking at a charming nearby farm. Though apples, grapes, and strawberries top the list in Northeast Ohio, hungry romantics can find every kind of fruit—from the smallest blueberry to the most sizable watermelon—ready to be picked on a pleasant, sunny morning.

Step by Step

10 A.M.: Strawberries are among the first of the summer fruit crops. When they appear in late May and early June, make plans to spend a morning at a pick-your-own farm. Why mornings? That's when the dew is still clinging to the fruit, before the hot sun of afternoon has a chance to affect these newly ripe berries.

Hilgert's runs just such a farm in Randolph on the southeast side of town. Owner Karen Hilgert typifies the spirit of the family farmer devoted to sharing the experience of farm life with the public. "We specialize in Ohio produce, and we really try to involve the customer," says Hilgert. Her farm has a pick-your-own strawberry patch. Simply take a basket, find a section heavy with shiny red strawberries, and set to work picking the fruit of the vine. Look for berries that are not too big, not too small, not too bright, and not too pale. Hungry eyes might make you overload yourself with strawberries, but not to worry, these berries freeze and preserve well. If stored properly, farm-fresh strawberries can last an entire summer.

Hilgert's also grows raspberries, tomatoes, and a host of other crops throughout the season.

NOON: Preparing your bounty is the other half of the fun. If you have a rocking chair at home, this is a good day to set it out on the porch, get out your paring knife and a colander, and get to work. Pit, slice, chop, and peel—together. There's something about spending a day in the country that will set you in an "Americana" kind of mood, so indulge (if you want to get really corny about it, slip a copy of Aaron Copland's *Appalachian Spring* in the CD player). You'll enjoy the fresh air—and so will curious neighborhood bees. Politely shoo them away while you plan your fruitful evening together.

If you have a rocking chair at home,
this is a good day to set it out on the porch,
get out your paring knife and a colander,
and get to work.

I'm a fanatic for pies. The smell of a freshly baked pie in the oven—with a fresh pint of ice cream lying in wait in the freezer—is a very sensuous experience. A savior for pie-lovers is the prepackaged pie crust. I follow this very simple recipe for pies and get fabulous results every time: Line a pie tin with a ready-bake crust, cover the tin with aluminum foil, and lay about 30 pennies atop the foil (this keeps the foil from flying away in your oven). Bake the crust for 30 minutes at 450 degrees, while you hull, cut, or chop your ingredients. Though my personal favorite is apple pie, you can use any hearty fruit for a filling (peaches, strawberries, blackberries, or raspberries will do just fine—or a mixture of your favorite fruits). Fill the baked pie crust till it's brimming with fruit, drizzle a half cup of honey over it, then sprinkle with a half teaspoon of nutmeg. Add the zest from the peel of half a lemon and arrange four to five tablespoon-sized pats of butter over the top of the

Hungry eyes might make you overload yourself with strawberries, but not to worry, these berries freeze and preserve well.

pie. Cover the pie with the second pie crust. Bake in the oven for about half an hour and let the pie set for an hour or two before you serve it. The result is a professional-looking pie that will impress the both of you.

Local farmers like Hilgert report that their customers return year after year for this ritual, one that you and your loved one might turn into an annual event.

Variations:

FARM-FRESH FROM CITY MARKETS: Though a trip to a family farm is fun, you can optimize your time—but still get the same quality—by traveling to a nearby organic or farmer's market. Here are a few to choose from.

SHAKER SQUARE MARKET: Run by Donita Anderson and Mary Holmes, this market includes only produce grown by Ohio farmers, and more than 50 percent of it is organic. "Chefs and foodies come first thing in the morning, followed by an eclectic mix of people from all over the city," says Anderson. Master gardeners are also there selling their harvest. The market is modeled after the Green Market in Manhattan.

NATURE'S BIN: In addition to selling fresh, delicious, and often organic foods, Nature's Bin hosts seasonal celebrations throughout the year.

When your favorite fruit is in season, you'll likely find a cornucopia of it at the Bin, along with recipes, tastings, and specials.

MILES FARMER'S MARKET: At the Miles Farmer's Market, fresh produce sits alongside fresh pies and gourmet foods. Leaf through the lettuce, ramble through the berries, and mingle with the people at the Miles Farmer's Market.

Directory

Hilgert's Berry Farm and Market
3431 Waterloo Rd., Mogadore
330-325-1405
HOURS/AVAILABILITY:
Hours are seasonal, please call.

Miles Farmer's Market
28560 Miles Rd., Solon
440-248-5222
HOURS/AVAILABILITY:
Mon–Fri 9 a.m.–8 p.m.,
Sat–Sun 9 a.m.–6 p.m.

Nature's Bin
2255 Lee Road, Cleveland Heights
216-932-2462
HOURS/AVAILABILITY:
Mon–Fri 9 a.m.–8 p.m.,
Sat 9 a.m.–7 p.m.,
Sun 10 a.m.–6 p.m.

Nature's Bin
18120 Sloane Ave, Lakewood
216-521-4600
HOURS/AVAILABILITY:
Mon–Fri 9 a.m.–8 p.m.,
Sat 9 a.m.–7 p.m.,
Sun 10 a.m.–6 p.m.

Shaker Square Market
Shaker Square, Shaker Heights
No phone
HOURS/AVAILABILITY:
Saturdays from Mother's Day through the 3rd Saturday in October 8 a.m.–1 p.m.

Outing 13
MUSIC LOVERS

Season: All ~ **Time:** 2–4 hours
Location: East/Any
Intimacy level: 3 ~ **Cost:** $$–$$$$
Advance planning: Some–a lot

What You'll Do

🏹 Prepare and attend a concert in your own backyard.

NOTE: *This outing requires you to hire area musicians to plan your own mini-concert. Because of their busy schedules, and to allow for rehearsal time, you might want to plan at least a month ahead.*

A romantic gesture can come in the form of a sweet serenade under the window, a melodic sonata while you dine at home, a surprise afternoon quartet in the backyard, or an exploration of the hallowed chambers where classical music is performed in Cleveland, often for free. Cleveland is home to some of the most talented musicians and aspiring music students in the world—and they're looking for work! This creates a vibrant scene for classical music fans who want to hear the very best musicians play the very best music.

Step by Step

PLANNING AHEAD: For what is sometimes a very modest fee, you can hire a single musician for an hour or a quartet for an extravagant evening.

Call the Cleveland Institute of Music or the Cleveland Music School Settlement. Both institutions can offer leads on students who are willing to play, for a price, music that you choose. These musicians have the magical ability to turn a ho-hum evening into a hum-along wonderland.

The musicians you hire can also help you pick a piece of music that is appropriate, alluring, and romantic. If you want a souvenir of your evening, take a trip to Educator's Music to purchase a copy of the sheet music, which helpful staff can assist in finding—if it's available. A talented calligrapher—call the Cleveland Institute of Art for a reference—can add an inscription to the cover sheet, and you can fill the insides of the covers with photos from your special evening.

5:30 P.M.: Hold the concert in your garden or in your living room. Make it a surprise and serve a light plate of cheese and paté, or even a proper English afternoon tea as the musicians play for you.

While such a concert might sound like it's only for the extravagance of young lovers or the soon-to-be-engaged, it is the perfect romantic gesture for a relationship at any age, and you'd be surprised at how little you might have to spend.

When the musicians have finished and you are alone together, present your guest with the personalized copy of the score from the day's performance.

Variations:

WORTH THE TRIP: Northeast Ohio's classical music scene is so vibrant, it's not necessary to limit yourself to Cleveland. It's worth the time and effort to get to Finney Chapel. Oberlin's school of music attracts top-

Hold the concert in your garden or in your living room. Serve a light plate of cheese and pate, or even a proper English afternoon tea as the musicians play for you.

notch students and faculty and such esteemed guest artists as the London Brass. The Oberlin Opera and the Oberlin Choristers chamber choir perform here to greatly appreciative audiences.

Stop in at the Fox Grape, a restaurant owned by Oberlin faculty members that is known around town as being "a place for intellectuals." Plan to eat before the concert, however, as Oberlin is a place that subscribes to the early-to-bed principle, and restaurants here close early.

Directory

Cleveland Institute of Music

11021 East Boulevard, Cleveland

216-791-5000

HOURS/AVAILABILITY:
Office: Mon–Fri 9 a.m.–5 p.m.

Cleveland Music School Settlement

11125 Magnolia Dr., Cleveland

216-421-5806

HOURS/AVAILABILITY:
Office: Mon–Fri 9 a.m.–7:30 p.m.

Educator's Music

13701 Detroit Ave., Lakewood

216-226-6780

HOURS/AVAILABILITY:
Mon–Tue 10 a.m.–7 p.m.,
Wed–Thu 10 a.m.–6 p.m.,
Fri–Sat 10 a.m.–5 p.m.

Finney Chapel

W. Lorain and Professor Streets, Oberlin

440-775-8169

HOURS/AVAILABILITY:
Concert times vary.

Fox Grape Cafe and Catering

19 West College St., Oberlin

440-774-1457

HOURS/AVAILABILITY:
Mon–Thu 8 a.m.–6 p.m.,
Fri–Sat 8 a.m.–10 p.m.

Outing 14
MOVIE AND A PIZZA—WITH A TWIST

Season: Spring, Summer, Fall
Time: 5 hours ~ **Location:** Downtown/East
Intimacy level: 1 ~ **Cost:** $$–$$$
Advance planning: Some

What You'll Do

🔷 Shop for fresh ingredients in an old-world market ($15–$20).

🔷 Bake a homemade pizza on the grill in the great outdoors.

🔷 Sprawl on the lawn at Cain Park for an evening of live entertainment ($10–$35).

NOTE: *You'll want to plan ahead for an evening when there's a concert you'd like to see at Cain Park, where performances are held all summer. You'll also need one of those small, inexpensive, drugstore grills to make this meal—Cain Park doesn't supply grills—and a pizza stone. But these supplies will come in handy for quick grilling throughout the year as you become thrilled with the taste of fresh-baked pizza. Also, order tickets ahead of time: Cain Park is small and popular—tickets can go fast. Also, no alcohol allowed here.*

izza and a movie. Again. Romance doesn't have to be grand, expensive, and outrageous, but most certainly, it should never get dull. Sometimes adding a slight, inventive twist to a familiar routine can be nearly as refreshing as a trip to the Mediterranean. And if you plan it well, you can turn that boring old pizza and a movie into an inventive, delicious night of romance and togetherness.

Step by Step

BEFORE YOU GO: Shop at Gallucci's for some spices and frozen pizza dough, a jar of sauce, cheese, and meat. If you've never been to Gallucci's, give yourself some time to prowl through its aisles filled with imported Italian foods and spices—you'll probably end up picking up a basketful of fresh and canned foods that just aren't available at your local grocer. Sumptuous sauces, crunchy biscotti, and a great selection of olive oils and balsamic vinegars will help you stockpile your pantry for months to come. When you get home, prepare and pack your picnic basket.

6 P.M.: Throw your picnic basket in the back seat and your grill in the trunk (don't forget tin foil for grilling the toppings, a pizza stone, and, of course, charcoal) and head to Cain Park. In the summertime, the park comes alive with concerts and plays of remarkable quality. A picturesque landscape of pathways, replica 1920s lamplights, and green, green grass, Cain Park is a lovely place to spend time. Get there early to prepare your dinner (you'll be glad you did—parking can sometimes be a problem around concert time).

Pick a quiet spot in the park for preparing your dinner. Bob Brown, head chef at Gamekeeper's Lodge in Rocky River, likes to grill his pizza over hot coals. He swears once you've had pizza off the grill, you'll battle the January sleet to avoid having oven-baked pizza again. Brown suggests first grilling your toppings—anything from onions to salmon will do. Once the grill is fired up, roast the veggies on tin foil over the warming coals. Set the defrosted pizza dough on the pizza stone. You might want to flavor the bottom of the pizza with a little olive oil and sprinkle the stone with some corn meal before setting it on the grill—it will keep the dough from sticking to stone. Cover the dough lightly with sauce and cheese. When the toppings are grilled, throw them on top of the prepared shell. Cover the grill and let the pizza bake over medium-to-high heat for about 10–15 minutes.

Dine in luxury on this most unique pizza pie, enjoying the warmth and sun, the pleasant evening breeze, and the company you're keeping.

8 P.M.: When you've finished eating, walk across the park to the theater area and find a spot to sit. If you're sitting on the seats be sure to bring along a comfy chair, a blanket or two, and a sheet of plastic to put under your blanket (Hefty bags are perfect for this) in case there's any moisture left in the ground from a recent shower. Outdoor theater and concerts offer plenty of opportunity for snuggling, so enjoy the show on this special midsummer's evening.

Variations:

CONCERT IN THE PARK: Every Sunday night at 7 p.m. from June to August, Lakewood Park comes alive with music—free music. Big bands, folk artists, and rock groups take the stage to perform at the park's band shelter just a few hundred yards from the shores of Lake Erie. Plenty of picnicking space is available, so you can grill a pizza at the park. Or, carryout pita pizzas, salads, and pita pocket sandwiches are easy to pick up at Aladdin's Eatery just up the street from the park.

Directory

Aladdin's Eatery
14536 Detroit Ave., Lakewood
216-521-4005

HOURS/AVAILABILITY:
Mon–Thu 11 a.m.–
10:30 p.m., Fri–Sat
11 a.m.–11:30 p.m.,
Sun 11 a.m.–10 p.m.

Cain Park
Superior and Lee Rds., Cleveland Heights
216-371-3000

HOURS/AVAILABILITY:
Concert times vary.

Gallucci's
6610 Euclid Ave., Cleveland
216-881-0045

HOURS/AVAILABILITY:
Mon–Fri 8 a.m.–6 p.m.,
Sat 8 a.m.–5 p.m., Sun closed

Lakewood Park
Lake Ave. and Belle Ave., Lakewood
216-521-7580 (City Hall)

HOURS/AVAILABILITY:
Concert times vary.

Outing 15

PUBLIC SQUARE AT THE HOLIDAYS

Season: Winter ~ **Time:** 4 hours
Location: Downtown
Intimacy level: 1 ~ **Cost:** $–$$$$
Advance planning: None

What You'll Do

➤ Take in the sights and sounds of the holidays on Public Square.

➤ Skate circles on Public Square ($5).

➤ Indulge in an extravagant meal at a gourmet restaurant ($80–$130).

Sure, sure, you've been there before. But have you really done Public Square at the holidays? Or were you in a hurry, frantically searching aisles of racks for just the right sweater, pushing past shoppers to get to the red-tag bargains? Did you walk by the ice skaters and think to yourself, I'm gonna do that next year?

Well, do it this year! The holidays are stressful enough, and it's a shame to let the season pass by without indulging in its beauty and charm. An afternoon walk through Public Square, a peep into Dillard's, or a long hot-chocolate break might be enough to satisfy your holiday cravings, but take it one step further. There is an art to enjoying this spectacle during the holidays, and the first objective is to include as little shopping as possible. For December transforms Public Square from a mere civic center to a magical kingdom that can only really be understood by small children—or adults in love.

Step by Step

6 P.M.: You must begin your day with a walk through Dillard's—but not for shopping, just to take in the sights. This lasting landmark housed the Higbee Company when it was built in 1931 as part of the Terminal Tower project. Back then, large department stores were located only in downtown areas and housed everything from specialty clothes to such oddities as gourmet foods, full-fledged toy departments, and even pets for sale—the department store of today is a different creature entirely. But the downtown Dillard's is still alive with sights, smells, decorations, and (thank goodness) staff at the height of the holiday shopping season. Walk in through the main doors and look upward, enjoying the elegant decorations and festive spirit of the store.

Next, step into the Avenue, but go to the upper level, away from the throngs of shoppers. This way, you can see directly into the Victorian balloons and colorful dirigibles that float high above the fountains. Descend to the fountain level where you'll likely run into a large nutcracker. Your adult self will tell you to avoid direct eye contact with him, but listen to your inner child daring you to pull the lever in his back. Engage him!

7 P.M.: Now you're ready for the Public Square ice-skating rink (at the northwest quadrant of the Square). From Thanksgiving to mid-January, in any weather, you can rent skates and twirl through this magical portion of the square. This tradition is relatively new to Public Square but very welcome. The rink is small enough that the skaters around you can't pick up too much speed—good news for skaters whose last excursion involved a 10 p.m. curfew. Skate rental is inexpensive as well, generally a paltry $1, in addition to a small entrance fee. Christmas carols issue from a sound system that looks like it was borrowed from the prop room at *M*A*S*H**, and the skating chalet offers hot chocolate and doughnuts to skaters and passersby.

8 P.M.: With wobbly ankles, walk up to the Renaissance Hotel lobby. I like to think of this space as the romantic epicenter of Cleveland, and I go there when I need a pick-me-up. Choose a seat near the *City of Culture* fountain. The marble of this fountain is reputed to have come from the same quarry as that used for Michelangelo's *David*. It,

and the reliefs that adorn the ceiling of the splendid room, will put you more in mind of an Italian castle than an urban American hotel. Glance out the window at Public Square as you sip a hot chocolate— or a hot toddy—ordered from the bar. If you're lucky, and if you wish very hard, a light snow might start to fall on the skaters and busy shoppers outside.

Still have some steam? Walk upstairs to Sans Souci for an unforgettable meal at an award-winning restaurant. Sans Souci specializes in Mediterranean fare, presenting delightfully crafted meals in a warm and charming atmosphere. Though it's a room for lovers, Sans Souci is one of the few places in Cleveland where you could dine alone and feel completely at home. The wall murals keep you company, and the sheltered alcoves of the place create a cozy atmosphere. You will not soon forget the experience. Usually, the menu features a lobster specialty of one sort or another, and if you're going whole hog on the holiday indulgence strategy, this is what you'll want to order.

At the end of this day you'll be in the mood to finish decorating the house and bask in the goodwill of the season. As they say, the season is all about giving—and that includes giving to yourself.

Variations:

NELA PARK: Another extravagantly romantic thing to do at the holidays is to take a drive through Nela Park to see the GE holiday lighting display at Nela Park. The display, which is lighted in early December, stays active from dusk to dawn through January 1. The Nela Park lights have delighted, amazed, and impressed Clevelanders since the

*If you're lucky,
and if you wish very hard,
a light snow might start to fall on
the skaters and busy shoppers outside.*

mid-1920s with everything from twinkling icicles to large-scale lighted holiday greeting cards to the community. If you can, wait till the late-night hours when the crowds die down, and you'll have less traffic to deal with as you drive through the site with Cleveland's biggest holiday electric bill.

Directory

The Avenue at Tower City
230 W. Huron Rd., Cleveland
216-771-0033

HOURS/AVAILABILITY:
Mon–Sat 10 a.m.–8 p.m.,
Sun noon–6 p.m.

GE Lighting Nela Park Holiday Display
1975 Noble Rd., Cleveland
216-266-2185

HOURS/AVAILABILITY:
Dusk–dawn

Renaissance Cleveland Hotel
24 Public Square, Cleveland
216-696-5600

HOURS/AVAILABILITY:
Lobby always open.

Sans Souci
24 Public Square, Cleveland
216-696-5600

HOURS/AVAILABILITY:
Mon–Fri 11:30 a.m.–
2:30 p.m.; Sun–Thu
5:30p.m.–10 p.m., Fri–
Sat 5:30 p.m.–11 p.m.

Outing 16

I COULD'VE DANCED ALL NIGHT

Season: Spring, Summer, Fall
Time: Up to 12 hours ~ **Location:** Downtown/West
Intimacy level: 1–3 ~ **Cost:** $$$–$$$$
Advance planning: None

What You'll Do

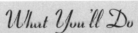

- Go on an all-night dancing rampage through the club scene ($40–$100).
- Fuel up on breakfast at a late-night eatery ($20).
- Watch the sunrise together.

NOTE: *Nights like this one never really seem to be planned; more often, they just happen. But if you can plan ahead, try to rest up the day before—and start your evening late.*

erhaps it's a rite of passage for young lovers to go out dancing all night, revive with breakfast at a late-night greasy spoon, then watch the sun rise together. If you subtract the greasy spoon from the equation, this is how Romeo and Juliet spent their first evening together. But on an inspired night, *any* of us can find a reason to indulge in this kind of folly. Of course, new love provides the much-needed adrenaline for such an outing; but it's open to any adventuresome souls willing to put in the time.

Step by Step

10 P.M.: Make a tour of the downtown dancing scene, starting at the Warehouse District's Velvet Dog where the crowd is young, dancers fill the floor, and loungers look on from cozy chairs and couches that dot the interior. Wish is the trendy next stop in the Warehouse District, touting a variety of dance music styles throughout the week. You could spend the entire evening just dancing through the warehouse district. Next, stop in at the Mercury Lounge where the ultra-hip dance beside curtains that give the bar an eerily retro atmosphere. Then walk down to the Blind Pig for some good, old-fashioned, live rock and roll or blues.

The crowd is young, dancers fill the floor, and loungers look on from cozy chairs and couches that dot the interior.

3 A.M.: Starving? At about 3 a.m., the Mardi Gras is just coming alive. On a weekend night, you might find a jazz band still playing amidst the noise of coffee cups clanking and the sound of forks scraping up scrambled eggs and hash browns. Late-night partyers fill the dimly lit bar looking for hot coffee, comfort food, and conversation before it's time to finally go home.

5:30 A.M.: If you've held out this long, ask the waitress at the Mardi Gras for a couple of coffees to go and a Danish or two and gear up for a romantic sunrise at Edgewater Park.

In early to mid-June, the sun will officially rise as early as 5:57 a.m., and the colors of dawn begin at least a half-hour before, accompanied by a morning bird-song serenade. Sip on your coffee, and enjoy the show.

Sunrises follow the same general rules as sunsets—an early morning rain can tame the flaming red hues of a sunrise, while a dry spell can enhance its intensity. In fact, you can judge the day ahead somewhat accurately by the old nautical nursery rhyme:

Red skies at night, sailors' delight
Red skies in morning, sailors take warning

Everyone should have an evening like this at least once in their lives. Going out all night dancing with someone special and then staying up to watch the sunrise is one of those experiences that you talk about the rest of your life. Though it takes some staying power, it's well worth staying up for.

Variations:

If you'd like to be closer to home for the sunrise, follow the recipe above for dancing but split off for the remainder of the evening by taking one of these two routes ...

WEST SIDE SUNRISE: West Siders like Michael's. The food is good, the location is convenient, and locals know the owner as "the guy who serves a free Thanksgiving meal to the homeless each year." Michael's is a comfortable place for an early-morning meal. Try to get a seat by the window if you can, to keep an eye on the sky. When it looks like it's close to sunrise, head to Valley Parkway, just over the Detroit Bridge leading to Lakewood. The first turn-off from Valley Parkway is Stinchcomb Hill, one of the higher points on the west side of town. At this peaceful place you'll have plenty of privacy for early-morning sunrise-gazing. Bring along a blanket for cuddling.

EAST SIDE SUNRISE: Michael's Diner at Shaker Square is a choice spot for early-morning eats. This diner has been a landmark "whistle stop" for years, plying early morning commuters with a quick coffee before they hop on the Rapid Transit. Following breakfast, head over to the easternmost of the Shaker Lakes, Upper Shaker Lake. In this serene setting, enjoy the first rays of dawn.

Sunrises follow the same general rules
as sunsets—an early morning rain
can tame the flaming red hues of a sunrise,
while a dry spell can enhance its intensity.

Directory

Blind Pig
1228 W. 6th St., Cleveland
216-621-0001
HOURS/AVAILABILITY:
Daily 5 p.m.–2:30 a.m.

Edgewater Park
8107 Lakeshore Blvd. (office), Cleveland
216-881-8141 (office)
HOURS/AVAILABILITY:
Daily dusk–dawn

Mardi Gras
1423 E. 21st St., Cleveland
216-566-9094
HOURS/AVAILABILITY:
Mon–Thu 11 a.m.–2:30 a.m.,
Fri–Sat 11 a.m.–5 a.m.,
Sun closed

Mercury Lounge
1392 W. 6th St., Cleveland
216-566-8840
HOURS/AVAILABILITY:
Daily 5 p.m.–2:30 a.m.

Michael's
19797 Detroit, Rocky River
440-356-1233
HOURS/AVAILABILITY:
Mon–Fri 6:30 a.m.–midnight,
Sat–Sun 24 hours

Michael's Diner at Shaker Square
13051 Shaker Blvd., Shaker Heights
216-752-0052
HOURS/AVAILABILITY:
Open 24 hours

Shaker Lakes
2600 S. Park Blvd., Shaker Hts.
216-321-5935
HOURS/AVAILABILITY:
Daily dusk–dawn

Velvet Dog
1280 W. 6th Street, Cleveland
216-664-1116
HOURS/AVAILABILITY:
Wed–Thu and Sat
7 p.m.–2:30 a.m.,
Fri 4 p.m.–2:30 p.m.

Wish Nightclub
621 Johnson Ave., Cleveland
216-902-9474
HOURS/AVAILABILITY:
Wed–Sat 5:30 p.m.–4 a.m.

Outing 17
NATURALLY SWEET

Season: Late Winter/Early Spring
Time: 3 hours ~ **Location:** Southeast
Intimacy level: 1 ~ **Cost:** $–$$
Advance Planning: None

What You'll Do

- Enjoy the late wintertime outdoors at Hale Farm and Village ($10–$30).
- Join in the harvest by stirring vats of bubbling sap.
- Indulge in all kinds of maple-sugary confections.

Sap. One of the sure signs that spring is on its way. According to the *Ohio Almanac*, the state of Ohio ranks in the top five nationally for maple sugar production. In February when the maple trees are tapped in Northeast Ohio, this part of the state becomes a hotbed of sugaring activity. The sweet reward of this slow process—maple syrup and maple candy—can best be tasted at a host of local seasonal festivals. The charming drive out to Hale Farm, a long walk among the stands of maples when the first hint of spring is in the air, and the smell of a wood fire burning under giant vats of sticky, sugary liquid can have a recharging effect on grumpy, winter-weary lovers.

Step by Step

9 A.M.: On Saturdays and Sundays from mid-February to mid-March,

Hale Farm welcomes guests for a re-creation of maple sugaring season the way it was back in the mid-1800s. If you grew up with the *Little House on the Prairie* books and television show, then you'll like this place. Hale Farm re-creates—very accurately—what life was like in that period, and the farmhands at Hale Farm take no shortcuts in their production process. As you begin your visit, first observe up close how trees are tapped. This is the beginning of a process that produces the sugar or syrup that once supplied a family's entire sugar requirement for a year.

As you walk through the farm, you can observe the process of maple sugaring, observing all the steps from the tapping of the trees to the sugar house system to the canning process.

9:30 A.M.: Stir things up. Throughout the morning, there are opportunities for the two of you to get involved. Trees need to be tapped, and buckets placed underneath to catch the sap. The buckets need to be looked after and emptied, vats of maple syrup need stirring, and there's lots of maple candy that needs to be eaten! The busy staff—dressed in period costumes—performs the tough chores necessary to produce maple syrup and sugar.

10:30 A.M.: Hard work calls for hearty food, and there's no shortage of pancakes and sausage smothered in Hale Farm maple syrup. Savor the taste of true maple syrup and vow to throw away that fake stuff in your refrigerator when you get back home.

After breakfast, visit the farm animals that call Hale Farm home. They might feel slightly neglected with all the farmhands out working on syrup production. Walking through this serene farm you can't help but think how hard—but rewarding—life was when most things were still made by hand. Take time to enjoy the peace and beauty of this place.

On your way out, pick up a tin or two of maple syrup to keep on hand through the rest of the winter and ask for some Fowler's Mill pancake mix—milled at Fowler's in Chardon.

When you are finally home, you may find you are both craving a little more sugar. If so, pop up a batch of popcorn together and have some midwinter's fun with the following recipe:

Maple Popcorn
1 tablespoon butter
1 cup maple syrup
3 tablespoons water
3 quarts popped corn

Boil butter, syrup, and water until the mixture forms a soft ball when a small amount is dropped from a teaspoon into a glass of cold water. Add 3 quarts popped corn. Stir briskly until mixture cools and coats the popcorn evenly. (Recipe courtesy of the Ohio Maple Producers Association.)

Variations:

GEAUGA, MAPLE SYRUP CAPITAL OF OHIO. Geauga County is the leading producer of maple syrup in Ohio. The many festivals here during sugaring season are testimony that they take their maple sugar seriously. During February and March you can't drive 10 miles without seeing a makeshift sign—or even a billboard—advertising this or that pancake breakfast or syrup festival.

The largest of the festivals, the Geauga County Maple Festival, takes place in Chardon every year in early April. The requisite pancakes and sausage breakfasts are augmented with hard and soft maple sugar candies, competitions for best syrups and sugars, and a host of demonstrations and hands-on activities designed to teach visitors more about the maple sugaring process—and to give volunteers a break from constant stirring.

Directory

Geauga County Maple Sugar Festival
Burton Square, Burton
440-286-3007
HOURS/AVAILABILITY:
Call for dates.

Hale Farm and Village
2686 Oak Hill Rd., Bath
800-589-9703
HOURS/AVAILABILITY:
Hours are seasonal, please call.

Outing 18
THE SWING-SHIFT DATE

Season: Spring, Summer, Fall
Time: 5 hours ~ **Location:** East
Intimacy level: 1–2 ~ **Cost:** $$–$$$
Advance planning: Some

What You'll Do

➤ Dine under the stars for an unusual nighttime picnic.

orking odd hours can be difficult on romance. Many relationships have buckled under the pressure of trying to make time together. Conflicting shifts or even a high incidence of after-work obligations can keep a couple apart. But couples who can be creative about juggling awkward schedules and shifts might find that their time together, though still limited, is more meaningful; and some go to great lengths to make this happen.

One Clevelander found the perfect romantic solution to this quandary. Kent Smith, executive director of Euclid Community Concerns, was smitten with a woman who worked the 3 to 11 shift. Their schedules made it hard to find time together, so Smith threw in the towel one evening, picked her up from work, and took her to Wade Park Oval for a picnic, complete with candles, china, and a tasty meal.

"It's really fabulous to sit out in the evening like that, under the stars with some candlelight," says Smith. Of course, Wade Oval is not the safest place to be late at night armed with only a butter knife. However, as Smith recalls, "the cops stopped by, and once they saw that we were simply having a picnic, they looked at us funny but left us alone."

The novelty of planning such a picnic is surpassed only by the enjoyment you'll experience while on it, so start planning now to surprise your night-owl date.

Step by Step

2:30 P.M.: Evenings suggest more formal supplies than paper and plastic. Ford Restaurant Supply carries everything from tiny egg whisks to large industrial-sized stock pots. Ford's has an additional advantage: deep discounts. Face it—you're on an evening picnic, something's going to get dropped; you'll be a lot happier if it's a fifty-cent plate instead of wedding china from your Aunt Marge.
Take note that Ford's is quite a departure from the neighborhood Williams-Sonoma; there are no nice clerks in aprons preparing samples for you. In fact, you might want to bring your own flashlight to see in the darkened aisles, but a walk through this restaurant graveyard of plates, silverware, candlesticks, and serving dishes usually turns up all you'll need for your excursion, and maybe a gem or two that you weren't expecting. If you enjoy secondhand shopping, Ford's is well worth the trip for such staples as pots and pans as well as accessories like martini glasses, large serving platters, and vintage appliances of every size and variety.

Stars twinkle above, breezes will play with the flames of your candles, and your date will be impressed by this romantic gesture.

Run through a checklist while you're still at Ford's. Make sure you have a fold-up bridge table, two comfortable folding chairs, and candlesticks to make the evening complete (citronella candles available at most drugstores keep away nighttime insects). A white linen tablecloth and napkins will complete your table nicely. If you don't have these things around the house, ask about them at Ford's. You now have the materials to set a table for two.

3:30 P.M.: Now for the food. Evening picnics cry out for formality in cuisine, too. You're going to a lot of trouble here, so arrange to pick up a meal at your favorite restaurant. Because of its proximity to such institutions as Case Western Reserve University, the Cleveland Clinic, and University Hospitals, Club Isabella has become accustomed to catering to people with eclectic tastes and late-night hours. Call ahead and tell them what you're planning, and the staff at Isabella's can suggest a good meal and have it waiting for you to pick up at the designated time. Choose a menu that's easy to serve, such as a fresh salad, roasted chicken (which is still good even if it's not piping hot), and rice. Keep it simple—and don't forget dessert.

11 P.M.: Pick up your dinner at Club Isabella and then pick up your date. Find a well-lit spot at Wade Oval that is secluded from street traffic and near the pond. Quickly set up your table, light the candles, and seat yourselves for a leisurely dinner. Stars twinkle above, breezes will play with the flames of your candles, and your date will be impressed by this romantic gesture. After you nibble on dessert, walk over to the edge of the pond to enjoy the quiet of the evening.

Variations:

FLY BY NIGHT: If Wade Park Oval is too adventuresome a destination for you. there are some safer locations for late-night picnics. Apartment rooftops are wonderful, to the accompaniment of James Taylor's "Up on a Roof" (extra points if you can play guitar and sing it to your date). Smaller suburban parks are generally safe, but you run the risk of discovery by the local authorities, and most parks close around dusk, or at 11 p.m.

Directory

Club Isabella
2025 University Hospital Dr., Cleveland
216-229-1177
HOURS/AVAILABILITY:
Mon–Fri 11:30 a.m.–3:30 p.m., Mon–Thu
5:30 p.m.–11 p.m., Fri–Sat
5:30 p.m.–midnight

Ford Restaurant Supply
3815 Clark Ave., Cleveland
216-631-4900
HOURS/AVAILABILITY:
Mon–Fri 9 a.m.–5 p.m.,
Sat 10 a.m.–2 p.m.

Wade Park Oval
Martin Luther King Blvd., Cleveland
No phone
HOURS/AVAILABILITY:
Daily dusk–dawn

Outing 19

THE COUPLE THAT COOKS TOGETHER

Season: Any ~ **Time:** 4–5 hours
Location: Downtown
Intimacy level: 1–2 ~ **Cost:** $$
Advance planning: None

What You'll Do

- Shop together for ingredients at the West Side Market ($20–$40).
- Cook a labor-intensive yet rewarding meal together.
- Enjoy the fruits of your labor.

My parents used to cook together. Each had a specialty and a job to do at the family hearth. My father was great with twice-baked potatoes and tossed salads; my mother was fabulous with, well, everything else. I loved watching their silent rituals in the kitchen. Cooking for six children and frequent guests had developed their culinary routine into a kind of ballet with spatulas. Growing up in such a household, I believe that a couple that happily shares this chore will do well together—after all, cooking is something that must be done at least twice every day. If you can spend time together cooking happily, you're spending time together well.

Romney and Kate Cullers think so too. They reaffirm their love through a hauntingly romantic dish: risotto. This labor-intensive meal is perfect for two to cook and eat together. It's simple to make—if you have patience—and provides plenty of time for the togetherness.

Step by Step

2 P.M.: To market, to market. The first step in cooking is fresh ingredients, which means shopping. If you go alone, you accomplish the task quickly. If you shop with someone else it takes longer, but you have more fun. If you don't believe me, trail a couple in the grocery store and catch some of the debates that occur in front of confusing displays of pasta or along the snack aisle. You'll be surprised at the quick insight you'll gain into the dynamics of a relationship as young couple battles over rotini versus linguine no. 2, or the benefits of Pecan Sandies over Snackwells.

For this meal, begin at the West Side Market. Here you'll find many small shops under one lofty roof (the large space offers winter shoppers the feel of an open, outdoor marketplace) and all the ingredients you'll need. The owners of these small shops take a personal interest in your meal—and can act as referees when your food debates get out of hand.

"You stir the risotto, add a little wine, talk for a bit, drink a little wine ..." This recipe must work magic.

Because risotto has so many possibilities, you can meander through the vegetable stands, deciding which are most in-season and negotiating for only the best specimens. Inside the main hall of the market, browse through the meats and fish and decide what you might like to throw in. Shellfish is recommended for this dish for two reasons: it cooks well in the broth of the risotto, and it's widely believed to be an aphrodisiac. Peruse the offerings at S&S Seafood (stands D-1 and E-1) or Navillus Fish (stand F-11). Saffron can be found at Asian Spice (stand E-11). Of course, you'll need to purchase Italian arborio rice, available at Mediterranean Imported Foods.

For wine, walk over to Athens Pastries & Imported Foods. Though the selection is limited, while you're there you can also pick up a delicious sweet for dessert.

5 P.M.: Now you're done shopping and ready to cook. The key to risotto is stirring. Once you've started the risotto, it is imperative to stir, stir, stir, for at least 45 minutes, adding chicken stock—and wine—intermittently. As Romney Cullers puts it, "You stir the risotto, add a little wine, talk for a bit, drink a little wine . . ." This recipe must work magic. The Cullers used to make this recipe on dates; now they're cooking the same dish under their own marital roof.

Below is the Cullerses' own recipe for risotto they swear tastes better when prepared by two. It is my opinion that risotto cooks better when accompanied by a Puccini opera. *Turandot* and *Tosca* seem to provide the appropriate acoustic environment for the rice to bloom. If you're going for a more festive flavor, you can also try the Gypsy Kings' CD *Allegra*—its rhythms and harmony will add snap and flavor to the meal.

Romney Cullers's Romantic Risotto:
6 tablespoons butter
3 tablespoons finely chopped onions
1 garlic clove
2 cups arborio rice
Salt and freshly ground pepper to taste
1 teaspoon chopped stem saffron
5 cups chicken stock
1–2 cups dry white wine
1–4 cups grated Parmesan cheese

Heat 2 tablespoons of the butter in a fairly large, heavy pan. Add the onions and garlic and cook until onions are wilted. Add the rice, salt, pepper, and saffron and stir until the grains have a golden color.

Add the wine and cook, stirring, until the wine is evaporated.

Add the stock in increments of 1–2 cups at a time, stirring until all the liquid is absorbed, and repeating the process at intervals of 3–4 minutes—throwing in some wine every once in a while for good measure, says Cullers. Trade off the chore of stirring.

Risotto cooks better when accompanied by a Puccini opera. "Turandot" and "Tosca" seem to provide the appropriate acoustic environment for the rice to bloom.

When you're down to the last cup of stock, add in any meat, fish, or vegetables you choose. The Cullerses suggest an array of shrimp, mussels, and scampi. When all the liquid has been absorbed, fold in the remaining butter and cheese. Serve immediately.

Variations

TOSS A SALAD: On muggy summer nights, a romantic mood can quickly turn into aggravation over a hot stove. Indulge in a crunchy, flavorful summer salad instead—but not just an average salad. Walk through your favorite market together, choosing the most desirable vegetables to throw in, then shop for upscale items you don't normally incorporate in your everyday toss—smoked salmon, pine nuts, arugula, gourmet bean sprouts. When you get home, washing the vegetables will cool you down, and the chore of chopping and dicing the vegetables will go fast with both of you doing the work. Top it off with a light and tangy vinaigrette, then eat outside. By the time you're finished, you should be able to catch an evening breeze or two.

Directory

Athens Pastries & Imported Foods

2545 Lorain Rd., Cleveland

216-861-8149

HOURS/AVAILABILITY:
Mon–Sat 8:30 a.m.–6 p.m.

Mediterranean Imported Foods

1975 W. 25th St., Cleveland

216-771-4479

HOURS/AVAILABILITY:
Mon and Wed 8 a.m.–4 p.m.,
Fri–Sat 8 a.m.–6 p.m.

West Side Market

1995 West 25th St., Cleveland

216-664-3386

HOURS/AVAILABILITY:
Mon and Wed 7 a.m.–4 p.m.,
Fri–Sat 7 a.m.–6 p.m.

Outing 20
THE GETAWAY

Season: Any ~ **Time:** Overnight
Location: East
Intimacy level: 3 ~ **Cost:** $$$–$$$$
Advance planning: Some–A lot

What You'll Do

❧ Dine and spend the night at the Baricelli Inn ($125–$150).

❧ Wander through the galleries and shops in Little Italy.

❧ Enjoy a serenade by strolling musicians at a local gathering place ($20–$30).

NOTE: *Because the Inn is in such high demand, you may want to call at least a month in advance to schedule this special evening.*

*Y*ou don't necessarily have to leave town to feel as if you've had a relaxing vacation. The American Association of Travel and Tourism reports that short weekend trips are replacing the traditional two-week-vacation model. Americans are looking for a quick getaway, a day or two of relaxation not far from home. Keeping close to home cuts down your travel time, allowing more time for relaxed togetherness in a beautiful urban setting.

Notable among those in the Cleveland area is the Baricelli Inn. This charming brownstone mansion-turned-inn, reminiscent of an Italian villa, boasts seven private guest rooms and a four-star restaurant run by chef and owner Paul Minillo.

Step by Step

4 P.M.: Settle into your room and take a walk through the Inn and around the garden in back, meeting Inn guests and chatting with the hotel staff.

5 P.M.: Take a leisurely walk around Murray Hill, where you can discover the Hill's many art galleries and shops. Notable galleries include the Bockrath Gallery, which features a fine collection of local and national artists represented in media from screen prints to oil paintings. The Avante Gallery carries artwork from the serious to the whimsical.

Some of the real treasures of Murray Hill aren't what you'd consider fine art. Take Presti's doughnuts for instance. Take a dozen. These doughnuts are a delightful, sugary diversion.

Continue along Mayfield Road, observing turn-of-the-century buildings built by Italian immigrants with Italy in mind. Just a block away on Mayfield Road, Holy Rosary Catholic Church—a must-see for any Little Italy tourist—is among the most ornate churches in Cleveland. This mixture of Romanesque and neoclassical architecture features a statue of Our Lady of the Holy Rosary, flanked by statues of Matthew, Mark, Luke, and John. Inside, a bas-relief of the Last Supper is a sight to behold—and a reminder that it's almost dinnertime.

6 P.M.: Back at the Baricelli, take a brief rest and prepare yourself for an unforgettable meal. Chef Paul Minillo prides himself on blending traditional recipes from back home with contemporary trends and in-season foods. Fresh herbs from the garden just outside the Inn add an unmistakable flair to the meals at the Baricelli.

8 P.M.: After dinner, walk back to the Hill and stop in at La Dolce Vita for an after-dinner drink at the bar, where food meets entertainment. In addition to serving up relatively upscale Italian food, Terri Tarantino—the proprietor at La Dolce Vita—dishes up very interesting entertainment on weekends. Depending on what night you go in, you can hear strolling mariachis, a violin-and-accordion duo, Flamenco dancers, or operatic arias. On summer evenings, Tarantino's staff opens the doors wide and sets up the outdoor patio, adding to the flair of this charming neighborhood place. Well fortified with good desserts, drinks, and music, head back to the Baricelli for an evening's rest.

9 A.M. (NEXT DAY): If you like, get up early the next day and take in at least one of the museums in University Circle. If the Baricelli has you nostalgic for a bygone era, stop at the Western Reserve Historical Society's Crawford Auto-Aviation Museum, where nearly 200 automobiles, aircraft, motorcycles, bicycles, and race cars are on display.

If cars don't catch your interest, consider walking through Lake View Cemetery, where beautifully kept gardens surround monuments to some of Cleveland's most important citizens. Set on 200 acres of high land, this serene place is like a boardroom for the prominent deceased of Cleveland society. The James A. Garfield Memorial sits high on a hill overlooking Lake Erie. A marble statue of the slain president graces a room that features a tower dome above and houses a crypt below. John D. Rockefeller, the Van Sweringen brothers (who were responsible for, among other things, the Terminal Tower), and Jeptha Wade, who made his fortune in the telegraph industry, are also buried here. Wade Memorial Chapel was designed by the same architects who built the Cleveland Museum of Art; the large stained glass window you see upon entering the memorial is a Tiffany original depicting fulfillment of the divine promise.

Depending on what night you go in, you can hear strolling mariachis, a violin-and-accordion duo, Flamenco dancers, or operatic arias

Variations:

PUTTIN' ON THE RITZ: No doubt, the Ritz-Carlton is one of Cleveland's most luxurious hotels. It is also the place legendary Cleveland rock and roll deejay Billy Bass believes is the most romantic spot in town. Four-star, award-winning service and impeccable attention to detail make this one of the more luxurious getaways available to Clevelanders. On weekends, when the business travelers go home, the Ritz offers specials and packages designed to lure suburbanite couples downtown for a night or two of sheer elegance. Call ahead and ask a reservation clerk about theater or spa packages, and book yourselves into the hotel for a weekend of self-indulgent luxury, such as a joint visit to Maxelle's, where a facial and rubdown will help you leave the stress of the week behind. Refreshed, dine at the Riverview Room in the hotel and take in the downtown scene—or simply enjoy the luxury and comfort available to you in your hotel room. Most importantly: Relax.

Directory

Avante Gallery
2062 Murray Hill Rd., Cleveland
216-791-1622
HOURS/AVAILABILITY:
Wed—Sat noon—5 p.m.

Baricelli Inn
2203 Cornell Rd., Cleveland
216-791-6500
HOURS/AVAILABILITY:
Mon—Sat 5 p.m.—11 p.m.;
Reservations required.

Bockrath Gallery
2026 Murray Hill Rd., Cleveland
216-721-5990
HOURS/AVAILABILITY:
Tue—Sat 11 a.m.—5 p.m.,
Sun 1 p.m.—5 p.m. and by appointment

Crawford Auto-Aviation Museum
10825 East Blvd., Cleveland
216-721-5722
HOURS/AVAILABILITY:
Mon—Sat 10 a.m.—5 p.m.,
Sun noon—5 p.m.

Holy Rosary Catholic Church
12021 Mayfield Rd., Cleveland
216-421-2995
HOURS/AVAILABILITY:
Tours by appointment only

La Dolce Vita
12112 Mayfield Rd., Cleveland
216-721-8155
HOURS/AVAILABILITY:
Mon Opera Night,
call for reservations;
Tue—Thu 5:30—11 p.m.,
Fri—Sat 11:30 a.m.—3 p.m. and
5:30 p.m.—1 a.m.,
Sun 4 p.m.—10 p.m.

Lake View Cemetery
12316 Euclid Ave., Cleveland
216-421-2665
HOURS/AVAILABILITY:
Daily 7:30 a.m.—5:30 p.m.
Call for special events.

Maxelle's
Tower City, Cleveland
216-621-4600
HOURS/AVAILABILITY:
Mon—Sat 9 a.m.—8 p.m., Sun
closed; call ahead for booking.

Presti's Bakery
12101 Mayfield Rd., Cleveland
216/421-3060
HOURS/AVAILABILITY:
Sun—Thu 6 a.m.—6 p.m.,
Fri—Sat 6 a.m.—10 p.m.

Ritz-Carlton Hotel
1515 West 3rd St., Cleveland
216-623-1300
HOURS/AVAILABILITY:
Call for room rates and
availability.

Outing 21

THE WATERFALL DATE

Season: Any ~ **Time:** 6 hours
Location: East
Intimacy level: 1 ~ **Cost:** $$–$$$
Advance planning: Some

What You'll Do

- Dine in a charming restaurant in Chagrin Falls ($50–$80).
- Take an after-dinner stroll to the falls.
- Dance the evening away ($25–$50).
- Grab a late-night snack ($10–$20).

It's the most charming town in Cuyahoga County, winter, spring, summer, or fall. Make a plan to visit Chagrin Falls with an eye for detail. The town is host to tourists throughout the year and offers heaping amounts of picturesque romance.

Step by Step

6 P.M.: A jaunt to "the Falls" must begin with the proper outfit. Get dressed up in your favorite casual dress and make an adventuresome first stop at Stix for a drink and an appetizer. The babyback ribs at Stix are difficult to eat only because as you pick them up, the succulent meat is already falling off the bone, dripping with the restaurant's tangy barbecue sauce.

6:45 P.M.: If you've made it through appetizers without dripping sauce on your blazer, pat yourself on the back and head for Gamekeeper's Tavern for your main course. You'll feel like you've just stepped into a hunter's lodge when you walk into this place. It's warm, comfortable, and filled to the ceilings with tools of the hunting trade. You'll know why when you look at the menu. Ostrich, alligator, and venison all appear on the menu alongside less adventuresome but equally tasty dishes like steaks and chicken. Taste some of the oddities at Gamekeeper's, if you're of a mind to, reminding yourself that variety is the spice of life.

8:30 P.M.: If you can, tear yourself away from the atmosphere at Gamekeeper's and take a short walk.

At night these falls on the Chagrin River—the centerpiece of this bucolic town—are lit with elegant care. It's hard to say what's more romantic—walking along the pathway by the falls or watching other couples, young and old, do the same. Though neither the highest nor the most roaring falls in Northeast Ohio, these are probably the most recognized and best-loved falling waters we have. Take time as you listen to the roaring water to enjoy this peaceful moment.

9:30 P.M.: Rick's Cafe is the neighborhood after-dinner spot for dancing. Here, you can kick up your heels to the sounds of local bands and catch the buzz of the nightlife. Rick's is the meeting place for locals, and everybody knows everybody here. If you listen closely you'll catch some good gossip as the evening's libation loosens local lips. But mostly, people come to Rick's to relax, have fun, and dance, so move out onto the dance floor and boogie until you're hungry again. You have one more stop.

11 P.M.: A romantic evening is incomplete without a late-night stop at Yours Truly. Yours Truly has earned a reputation for mixing up some of the best home-style cooking in town and for creating restaurants that emulate the feel of Mom's breakfast nook.

Variations:

AN AMBITIOUS WATERFALL TOUR: Pick a sunny afternoon, grab a road map, and prepare for a whirlwind, triple-play waterfall tour. Start your journey in Cuyahoga Falls, where the rolling waters create atmosphere in this quintessential Midwest town. Stop at Swenson's, an old-fashioned drive-up burger shack where the waiters and waitresses come out to the car to serve you. Get a Galley Boy burger, a couple of orders of onion rings, and some chocolate shakes to go, then head off to your next stop

Located in a more rural setting, Brandywine Falls is one of the prettiest stops on the Cuyahoga Valley National Recreational Area Towpath Trail. Linger here in the wilderness just long enough to take in these falls, comparing them with the Cuyahoga Falls and anticipating your next stop, Chagrin Falls. If you time it correctly, you'll arrive in Chagrin Falls in time for dinner, so follow the itinerary above—if you have the energy.

Directory

Gamekeeper's Tavern
87 West St., Chagrin Falls
440-247-7744
HOURS/AVAILABILITY:
Mon–Thu 11:30 a.m.–
2:30 p.m. and 5:30 a.m.
–10 p.m., Fri–Sat
11:30 a.m.–2:30 p.m.
and 5 p.m.–11 p.m.,
Sun 4 p.m.–9 p.m.

Rick's Cafe
86 N. Main St., Chagrin Falls
440-247-7666
HOURS/AVAILABILITY:
Mon 11:30 a.m.–2:30 p.m.
and 5:30 p.m.–10 p.m.,
Tue–Fri 11:30 a.m.–2:30 p.m.
and 5:30–10 .m., Sat noon–
3 p.m. and 5:30–10 p.m.,
Sun 5 p.m.–9 p.m.

Stix
8777 E. Washington Street,
Chagrin Falls
440-543-7849
HOURS/AVAILABILITY:
Mon–Thu 5 p.m.–9:30 p.m.,
Fri 5 p.m.–10:30 p.m.,
Sat 11:30 a.m.–4 p.m.
and 5 p.m.–10:30 p.m.,
Sun 5 p.m.–9 p.m.

Swenson's
658 East Cuyahoga Falls Ave.,
Cuyahoga Falls
330-928-8515
HOURS/AVAILABILITY:
Sun–Thu 11 a.m.–midnight,
Fri–Sat 11 a.m.–1:30 a.m.

Yours Truly
30 N. Main St., Chagrin Falls
440-247-3232
HOURS/AVAILABILITY:
Mon–Sat 6:30 a.m.–11 p.m.,
Sun 7:30 a.m.–9 p.m.

Outing 22
THE THEATER AND LATE-NIGHT EATS

Season: Any ~ **Time:** 8 hours
Location: Downtown, Near West
Intimacy level: 1 ~ **Cost:** $$$–$$$$
Advance planning: Some

What You'll Do

- Beat the rush to the theater by planning early appetizers at Playhouse Square ($20–$30).
- Enjoy Cleveland's lively theater scene ($60–$200).
- Dine at a bustling late-night restaurant ($60–$150).

njoy an upscale night of theater at Playhouse Square. With their recent restorations, the five theaters that make up Playhouse Square are attracting some of the hottest Broadway tours as well as unique productions that range from ballet to modern dance, from Shakespeare to Sondheim.

Planning is the key to a relaxed, enjoyable evening at the theater. Choosing the right venue, the best show, good seats, and an appropriate locale for dinner well in advance will add an element of luxury to your outing. First, select a show that appeals to your taste—as well as that of your date. Because a night like this can get pricey, be sure you both will appreciate the show you're seeing. More popular shows will, of course, require planning months in advance, as tickets are often sold out quickly for more sought-after productions, good seats going first.

Good seats are essential to making the evening truly special, particularly if you don't venture out to the theater very often. Splurge on dress-circle seating, not only for the view but for the pure extravagance of it.

Step by Step

5:30 P.M.: Beat the parking garage lines and leave plenty of time for mingling before the show. Get a good parking space at the Playhouse Square garage and walk to Ciao Cucina for appetizers. Munch on a pre-theater snack as the lines begin to form for parking spaces outside.

7:30 P.M. (or 30 minutes prior to showtime): Walk back across the street to the theater, leaving time before the show to mingle in the lobby. Each of the five theaters that comprise Playhouse Square can brag about the grandeur of its entranceway—the State Theatre boasts the largest theater lobby in the world. While you're there, make sure to ascend one of the grand staircases that flank the lobby for a view from above. The Ohio Theatre, the Allen Theatre, and the Palace Theatre provide a complex grouping of lobbies that are now interconnected. On a busy night, you can stroll through all these lobbies, comparing their decor.

10:30 P.M.: Plan to have dinner after the show. Dining before the show can be a hurried and unpleasant experience as diners are crunched for time, and the wait staff is under pressure to serve everyone before the show. Dining after the show allows time for relaxation, and for conversation about the highs and lows of the evening's performance.
　　Two restaurants stand out as particularly good choices for a meal

The State Theatre boasts the largest theater
lobby in the world. While you're there,
make sure to ascend one of the grand staircases
that flank the lobby for a view from above.

after the show. Johnny's Downtown is less than a 10-minute drive through downtown, but be quick about it. Johnny's only serves until 11:30 p.m. on weekend nights (you can call the theater ahead of time to find out at what time the performance ends and plot your reservations accordingly). Johnny's dining room is elegant, and the food is award winning. The duck confit appetizer is a decadent delicacy, and the shrimp gnocchi in white sauce sends me running to confession the next day. But leave room to indulge in bananas Foster for dessert. The dining room at Johnny's is a perfect complement to an evening of theater—quiet enough to accommodate lively conversation but just abuzz enough to make you feel like you're in the heart of Broadway.

Dining after the show allows time for relaxation, and for conversation about the highs and lows of the evening's performance.

If the performance ends too late for Johnny's, make a reservation at Lola in Tremont, where dinner is served until 2 a.m., making Cleveland a more civilized place with each late dinner served. Lola, with its trendy crowd and highly stylized decor by local up-and-coming designer Chris Schramm, is a dynamic setting in which to find yourself after the theater. Cleveland's elite stops here for the late-night food and the atmosphere. The low lighting and pseudo art deco features give the place a speakeasy elegance.

Chef and owner Michael Simon prepares whimsical but elegant meals he likes to call "urban comfort food." The goat cheese wrapped in prosciutto with asparagus is a wonderful way to begin your meal. Follow it up with entrees that include such diverse items as a knuckle sandwich, fresh fish, and game specialties.

After dinner, drive home to create some theater of your own.

Variations:

BEYOND PLAYHOUSE SQUARE: Cleveland's theater scene is vibrant. Just down the street from the Square is the Cleveland Play House. The Play House has the distinction of being the oldest resident theater company in the country. Encompassing a group of theaters—the Brooks and Drury, and the Bolton Theater—the Play House was designed by the same architect responsible for Lincoln Center in New York. Not far from the Play House is another historic theater, Karamu House. Karamu has distinguished itself as the oldest American theater company producing plays by African American playwrights. On the near West Side, up-and-coming playwrights and actors work together in true off-Broadway fashion to produce original, contemporary works at the Cleveland Public Theater.

COMMUNITY THEATER GEMS: The intimacy of a small community theater can really bring a performance to life for the audience. Don't overlook some of Cleveland's smaller theaters when planning an evening out. Usually you can see a performance for around $10 that might very well leave you every bit as satisfied as if you had paid the big bucks downtown.

CLAGUE PLAYHOUSE. The rustic setting of this theater brings to mind the Barnstormers of days gone by. In the comfortable, intimate setting, you'll see lively productions of everything from Broadway musicals to serious dramas. The Moosehead Saloon matches the intimacy of the theater, and is the "regular" stop for post-production parties. The Moosehead boasts pub food galore, and if you're in the mood for indulging don't miss the hot pepper cheese sticks.

BECK CENTER. Arrive early at the Beck Center to allow time for browsing through the gallery space, which features local artists of note. Productions in the Beck Center's comfortable theaters run from the experimental to the acclaimed, following the tradition established by founding theatrical father Vincent Dowling. After the theater, enjoy a meal at the Rush Inn. Its location to the Beck Center (just across the street) means it can't be beat for convenience. There is a lot of charm packed into this small neighborhood joint. Lean back in high natural-wood booths while indulging in fresh sandwiches and hearty burgers. Beer is best at the Rush Inn when consumed directly from the bottle—this is not a Pilsner glass kind of place.

ENSEMBLE THEATRE. The Ensemble Theatre has a progressive agenda. The theater produces works by local playwrights and observes such occasions as Black History Month with unique productions. For an after-theater meal, theater-goers can travel a short distance to Coventry, where the high-end Hyde Park Grille serves up sizzling steaks and gourmet game in the most romantic of atmospheres. If you're in for more moderate prices—and calories—build your own burrito at Que Tal where the food is heavier on spice than fat.

Directory

Beck Center for the Arts
17801 Detroit Ave., Lakewood
216-521-2540
HOURS/AVAILABILITY:
Schedules vary.

Ciao Cucina
1515 Euclid Ave., Cleveland
216-621-8777
HOURS/AVAILABILITY:
Tue–Sun open at 5 p.m., closing time varies according to theater schedule

Clague Playhouse
1371 Clague Rd., Westlake
440-331-0403
HOURS/AVAILABILITY: Schedules vary.

Cleveland Play House
8500 Euclid Ave, Cleveland
216-795-7000
HOURS/AVAILABILITY: Schedules vary.

Cleveland Public Theatre
6415 Detroit Ave., Cleveland
216-631-2727
HOURS/AVAILABILITY: Schedules vary.

Ensemble Theatre
3130 Mayfield Rd., Cleveland Hts.
216-321-2930
HOURS/AVAILABILITY: Schedules vary.

Hyde Park Grille
1823 Coventry Rd.,
Cleveland Hts.
216-321-6444
HOURS/AVAILABILITY:
Mon–Thu 5 p.m.–9:45 p.m.,
Fri–Sat 5 p.m.–10:45 p.m.,
Sun closed

Johnny's Downtown
1406 West 6th St., Cleveland
216-623-0055
HOURS/AVAILABILITY:
Mon–Thu 11:30 a.m.–3 p.m.
and 5 p.m.–10:30 p.m.,
Fri 11:30 a.m.–3 p.m.
and 5 p.m.–11:30 p.m.,
Sat 5 p.m.–11:30 a.m.,
Sun 4 p.m.–9 p.m.

Karamu House
2355 E. 89th St., Cleveland
216-795-7070
HOURS/AVAILABILITY: Schedules vary.

Lola
900 Literary Rd., Cleveland
216-771-5652
HOURS/AVAILABILITY:
Tue–Thu 4 p.m.–1 a.m.,
Fri–Sat 4 p.m.–2 a.m.,
Sun 4 p.m.–11 p.m.

Moosehead Saloon
694 Dover Center Rd., Bay Village
440-871-7742
HOURS/AVAILABILITY:
Mon–Thu 11:30 a.m.–
11 p.m., Fri–Sat 11:30 a.m.–
midnight, Sun 12:30 p.m.–
10:30 p.m.

Playhouse Square Center
1501 Euclid Ave., Cleveland
216-771-4444
HOURS/AVAILABILITY: Schedules vary.

Que Tal
1803 Coventry Rd., Cleveland Heights
216-932-9800
HOURS/AVAILABILITY:
Mon–Thu 11 a.m.–10 p.m.,
Fri–Sat 11 a.m.–11 p.m.,
Sun noon–10 p.m.

Rush Inn
17800 Detroit Ave., Lakewood
216-221-3224
HOURS/AVAILABILITY:
Daily noon–2:30 a.m.

Outing 23

BALLROOM DANCING

Season: Any ~ **Time:** 5 hours
Location: West
Intimacy level: 1 ~ **Cost:** $$$–$$$$
Advance Planning: Some

What You'll Do

◆ A Friday evening dinner at White Oaks ($50–$80).

◆ Dance to a live band at a vintage ballroom ($8).

◆ Take a moonlit walk on the green.

NOTE: *If you want to brush up on your steps, take a ballroom dancing class, which can run anywhere from one evening to six weeks.*

*I*f anyone tells you it's out of fashion, they're wrong. Ballroom dancing is in—and it's cool. Just knowing the basic steps can turn you into a star at the next wedding you attend. It's a skill not unlike golf. Even if you're not into it, you're better off if you know the basics just in case. As with the game of golf, once you get the swing of it, you won't want to stop. Dancing cheek to cheek brings you closer together with the one you love, both literally and figuratively. In your living room or on the dance floor, sharing this activity will help keep your relationship in step.

If your steps are a bit rusty, invest in a six-week class with your sweetie, or even with a friend. Karen and James, a platonic pair I know, liked their course at Brecksville Community Center so much that they opted to take the advanced class as well. When they're practicing, they

become a parody of that old radio show *The Bickersons,* arguing over
who will lead, or who is responsible for messing the twosome up. But
I've seen them dance together and their classes paid off. The minute
they close their mouths, they can glide across the floor with grace and
ease. Many community centers offer ballroom dance instruction, teach-
ing the basic steps and dances that will make you and your partner the
hit of the dance floor at the next wedding you attend—or even at the
trendiest of dance clubs.

Choose a class offered in your neighborhood (so you'll be less likely
to "skip" class). Community centers often have inexpensive courses, and
you'll be able to meet other couples from your area that share your interest in dance.

Step by Step

7 P.M.: Plan to have dinner at White Oaks, a beautiful, old-fashioned
restaurant that overlooks—you guessed it—a stand of white oak
trees. In the summer, the lush greenery just outside the picture window at White Oaks looks like an enchanted forest, and in the winter—after a fresh snowfall—the picture is stunning. Inside, the atmosphere is old fashioned and slightly upscale. Dressed up for an
evening of dancing, you'll feel at home in the dining room here, sipping on a cosmopolitan. The cuisine is classic and includes duck
breast, tender selections of beef, and roast chicken. Dine lightly in
anticipation of an active night, but enjoy the meal and the view.

8:30 P.M.: Dancing at the Springvale Ballroom is much the same as it was
in the 1930s. Expansive hardwood floors, a stage for the band, and a
seating and dining area for the guests. In this country-club setting,
the Springvale re-creates the heyday of the big bands.

The decor is so authentic, says manager Lynn Strinad, that "it is
rumored that Superman changed in our phone booth, that's how old
it is." This place was home to the Canteens during World War II—
morale-building evenings out for the soldiers that featured a flurry
of stars of the day serving food and entertaining the soldiers.

Prior to the war, the Springvale had to survive Prohibition. The
addition of a more discreet bar in the lower levels of the place made
it easy for the owners to take advantage of their proximity to the
lake—and the lake's proximity to Prohibition-free Canada. Every
posh club of that day had its own speakeasy, and the Springvale was
no exception.

But now, says Strinad, there is a license for the liquor, and food
and music to go with it as well as live, swinging big bands. The

Springvale has been on a tear to get new blood into their ballroom, with some success. It is the place to go for romantics who want to experience big band the way big band should be experienced.

10 P.M.: Winded? Take a stroll out on the beautiful grounds and golf course that surround the Springvale. Take off your shoes and walk through the well-manicured turf, sip on champagne, then have your own moonlit dance together as the music drifts outside from the ballroom. In old movies, this is the scene where it all happens—leaving the dance, the couple finds a spot in the garden, and he asks her to marry him, or she confesses her love for him. Make your own magic under the skies.

As a rule, the more you go dancing, the better you'll feel, so start a tradition of ballroom dancing now with the one you love to ensure health and goodwill for years to come.

Directory

Springvale Ballroom
5781 Canterbury Rd., North Olmsted
440-777-0161
HOURS/AVAILABILITY: Dancing Fridays 8 p.m.–1 a.m.

White Oaks
777 Cahoon Rd., Westlake
440-835-3090
HOURS/AVAILABILITY:
Mon–Thu 5 p.m.–10 p.m.,
Fri–Sat 5 p.m.–11 p.m.,
Sun 4 p.m.–9 p.m.

Outing 24
DAY TRIP TO EASTERN EUROPE

Season: Any ~ **Time:** All Day
Location: Downtown, East, South
Intimacy level: 1–2 ~ **Cost:** $–$$
Advance planning: None

What You'll Do

❧ Breakfast in Slovenia.

❧ Pick up some romantic Eastern European music for your day.

❧ Lunch in Poland.

❧ Stroll through gardens representing European countries.

*B*ill Spellacy was a character. An Irish policeman with a heart of gold, and always a tall tale to tell. So when he proposed to take his nieces and nephews on a tour of the great cities of Europe (mind you, this is an Irish family—there were plenty of nieces and nephews), his brothers shook their heads and said he should ask his superiors to ease up on his hours. But Spellacy held fast to his plan. Together they would see Berlin, Poland, Seville, and even Rome! Of course, these all are Ohio cities, but Spellacy managed to pack the kids in the car for the trip of a lifetime, without crossing a single state line.

Spellacy was a true romantic. He realized that everyone dreams of a grand trip to Europe, and while not everyone can afford to foot the bill, we each have in us enough imagination to create our own getaway. Spellacy did all the time.

Richard J. Konisiewicz, president of the Cleveland Cultural Gardens and the former liaison for international affairs at city hall, has devised a grand scheme that allows a couple on a budget to experience the wonders of Europe in one activity-packed day in Cleveland.

Step by Step

8:30 A.M.: "You'll want to begin at Fanny's," says Konisiewicz. Fanny's is a Slovenian restaurant that opens early and offers a hearty breakfast that includes meaty sausages, eggs, fresh pastries, and plenty of coffee, all served in a comfy setting. This is the place where the two of you can plot out your day, a long and winding adventure through Cleveland's ethnic subcultures.

9:30 A.M.: Pick up a soundtrack for your Eastern European day together at the Cleveland Public Library's music section. "Get anything by Frankie Yankovic, the Polka King of Cleveland," suggests Konisiewicz. He adds, "Get some Mieczyslaw Fogg—he sings about life and love, winning and losing, it's very passionate." If you feel you can spare the time, stop in the foreign language book section for some picture books to take along on your trip. The Cleveland Public Library's foreign language collection is rivaled only by that of the New York City Public Library.

10:15 A.M.: Throw the books in the car, pop in a tape, and make your way to the Polka Hall of Fame. Cleveland's Slovenian community rallies around this singular treasure, which would not exist without the aforementioned Frankie Yankovic. Yankovic was the first polka artist to break the chains of "regionalism," taking his act across the country and his hits across the charts. Bubble machines and Lawrence Welk rode the crest of Yankovic's wave; his rise to fame is documented here amidst rare artifacts of the long-lived polka craze.

NOON: It's time for lunch. Konisiewicz swears that the sauerkraut meals cooked up at John's Cafe are the best . . . this side of Fleet Avenue. "The decor is intimate," says Konisiewicz. "And Gerri, the establishment's ever-present matron, will greet you in traditional Polish style, asking, 'vhat do you vant?'" Be warned, John's Cafe is in an obscure location on E. 52nd Street. Just keep going and look hard—you'll find it.

Bring your books into John's and page through the photos of Europe. By now, you should be intrigued by the mysteries of Eastern

Europe and ready to plan a trip there. This is the place to do it, and chances are there's someone in John's Cafe who can give you some pointers on what sights to see while you're there.

1:30 P.M.: Walk through the Cleveland Cultural Gardens. The seed for these gardens was planted back in 1916 with the introduction of the Shakespeare Garden. From there, each major ethnic group in Cleveland tilled, weeded, and planted a slice of land up and down Martin Luther King Jr. Boulevard (formerly called Liberty Boulevard), creating about 25 garden spots. (The number varies to reflect changes in international politics, as shown by the recent tussle over garden space between the Serbian, Slovenian, and Croatian gardens.) In all, you can walk about two miles through the garden, taking a leisurely couple of hours to do so. Konisiewicz suggests that the most romantic spaces can be found in the upper level of the Hungarian Garden and in the Renaissance Garden.

Konisiewicz, a tireless enthusiast, would find 12 more things to do in this day he's created. No doubt if you traveled Cleveland's Europe with him for a day, you'd wind up on an inspired journey through the heart of a Cleveland you never knew was there.

Directory

Cleveland Cultural Gardens
Martin Luther King Jr. Blvd., Cleveland
No phone
HOURS/AVAILABILITY: Daily dawn–dusk

Cleveland Public Library
325 Superior Ave., Cleveland
216-623-2800
HOURS/AVAILABILITY:
Mon–Sat 9 a.m.–6 p.m.,
Sun 1 p.m.–5 p.m.

Fanny's
353 East 156th St., Cleveland
216-531-1231
HOURS/AVAILABILITY:
Mon–Sat 7 a.m.–8 p.m.,
Sun 11:30 a.m.–7 p.m.

John's Cafe
3658 E. 52nd St., Cleveland
216/641-3671
HOURS/AVAILABILITY:
Tue–Sat 11:30 a.m.–7 p.m.,
Sun noon–6 p.m.

Polka Hall of Fame
291 E. 222nd St., Euclid
216-261-3263
HOURS/AVAILABILITY:
Mon, Thu, Fri noon–5 p.m., Tue
3 p.m.–7 p.m.,
Sat 10 a.m.–2 p.m.

Outing 25

THE CLASSIC PICNIC

Season: Spring, Summer, Fall

Time: 2 hours ~ **Location:** East

Intimacy level: 1 ~ **Cost:** $

Advance Planning: Some

What You'll Do

🏹 Rent a Saab convertible.

🏹 Prepare a classic American picnic.

🏹 Scout out the perfect picnic spot at Punderson State Park.

🏹 Row on Punderson Lake.

The classic American picnic: a sunny day, white linen clothes, grass blowing in the breeze, you and your honey sitting side by side, lazily enjoying the day. "Standard picnic fare" will not do for this romantic outing. Simple, hearty foods will be the order of the day. And add nice touches like a white linen tablecloth, and real wineglasses instead of paper cups, and dress in comfortable elegance. These simple afternoons are often our fondest memories. You can never have enough of them. So create a memorable picnic for you and your loved one.

Step by Step

BEFORE YOU GO: Reserve a convertible. As my sister-in-law says, "I'll let your brother rent an extravagant car every once in a while. Better to part with $100 here and there than have him come home one afternoon having spent $50,000."

Provided they're in stock, you can rent a Saab convertible from Ed Wolfe Shaker Saab. The day before you plan to go on your picnic, call the store's owner, Jim Levine, to reserve a car. Traditional rental agencies generally have a convertible or luxury car available as well. I recommend the Saab for this special picnic.

10 A.M.: Prepare a picnic meal. Pack an appetizer of French bread and your favorite cheese in your picnic basket. Snap the ends off fresh green beans and bring along some balsamic vinegar and slices of tomato to toss in at the last minute.

For the main course, roast a chicken. To prepare the chicken, wash it well and salt and pepper it to taste. Add a few sprigs of fresh rosemary and a tablespoon of cumin for flavor. Quarter an orange and stuff it into the cavity of the chicken. In a Dutch oven prepare a large chopped onion and three stalks of chopped celery. Place the chicken over the celery and onion and drizzle with about ¼ cup olive oil and ¼ cup of white wine. Cover tightly and roast for 1 hour at 425 degrees. Serve fresh fruit for dessert.

1 P.M.: The two of you, picnic basket in hand, can jump into the car and enjoy the drive to Punderson Lake State Park; with its mansion, lake, and rolling tracts of land, Punderson is a charming spot for a summer country picnic. Located in Geauga County, this park is named for one of that county's early settlers, Lemuel Punderson, and is home to Punderson Lake, Ohio's deepest and largest glacial lake. The old Punderson Manor House, a charming structure built at the beginning of the century, is open to the public for tours.

*Rent a rowboat at the boathouse
and slowly meander toward a spot
right in the middle of the lake, where
you can drift aimlessly for a while.*

2 P.M.: For some post-lunch leisure, rent a rowboat at the boathouse and slowly meander toward a spot right in the middle of the lake, where you can drift aimlessly for a while. Listen for the sounds of birds chirping, fish surfacing, and children playing in the distance. Aren't Ohio summers wonderful?

Variations:

PORTAGE LAKES: The Portage Lakes area south of Cleveland is another wonderful spot for a picnic. This haphazard grouping of lakes has 37 miles of shoreline that offer a driving tour through beautifully kept country. Start your tour at Portage Lakes State Park, where you can view a map of the trails and roads that comprise the Portage Lakes area. Choose a path that the two of you like, and walk or drive around the lakes; you're guaranteed a beautiful view. But watch out for ducks. They're friendly, but hungry for tourist food.

Directory

Ed Wolfe Shaker Saab
10299 Shaker Blvd., Cleveland
216-231-2722

HOURS/AVAILABILITY:
Mon and Thu 9 a.m.–9 p.m.,
Tue, Wed, and Fri 9 a.m.–
6: p.m., Sat 9 a.m.–5 p.m.

Portage Lakes State Park
5031 Manchester Rd., Akron
330-644-2220

HOURS/AVAILABILITY:
Daily dusk–11 p.m.

Punderson State Park
11755 Kinsman Rd., Newbury
440-564-9144

HOURS/AVAILABILITY:
Daily dawn–dusk

Outing 26

A TALE OF TWO HAYRIDES

Season: Fall ~ **Time:** 3 hours
Location: South
Intimacy Level: 1 ~ **Cost:** $$–$$$
Advance planning: Some

What You'll Do

- Bundle up and pack a picnic basket full of snacks ($30).

- Climb aboard a horse-drawn or tractor-pulled hay cart ($125–$135).

- Catch a glimpse of the autumn moon through the smoke of a bonfire while sipping on a mug of warm cider.

NOTE: *Before you go, make sure that everyone in your party is allergy-free, dress warmly in layers, and take care to wear a good pair of boots. Unpaved country roads can be muddy, and nothing can ruin an evening like a pair of soaked socks. Both of the following locations for hayrides offer places to eat, but you have to bring your own food. Stock up on graham crackers, Hershey's chocolate bars, and marshmallows—the key ingredients for the childhood favorite, "smores." A few jugs of cider and a dozen doughnuts will come in handy during the evening as well.*

In Cleveland, the ever-burgeoning urban areas quickly give way to sprawling country scenes. You needn't drive more than a half-hour to get from the center of the city to the rural heartland. There, in the country towns, you can take in all the delights of fall, chief among them the age-old hayride. While some folks say spring is fleeting, I say fall is even more so. Autumn is our last chance to savor the weather before the onslaught of snow and slush. Indian summers bring out a sense of *carpe diem* in Ohioans, a last-ditch effort to welcome the warmth before the cold sets in. Take advantage of just such an autumn day for an unforgettable adventure in the woods.

There are still a few parks and family-owned farms that operate hayrides from the end of August through the end of November. They fill up big carts with stacks of sweet-smelling hay, hitch the wagon to a team of horses—or the more modern tractor—and pull you through the hearty fall air for a few miles of pure bliss.

Step by Step

7 P.M.: Dress yourselves in layers for a hayride, making sure you're warm and your feet will stay dry. Then prepare a basketful of goodies. Here is a list to start with, but add your favorite junk food as you go:

> A large Thermos full of hot chocolate or warm cider
>
> Graham crackers, Malley's chocolate bars, and marshmallows for smores
>
> Candy corn
>
> Doughnuts
>
> Apples
>
> Popcorn balls
>
> Handi-wipes

8 P.M.: Arrive at Meadow Ridge Farm or Spring Mist Farms. These two farms are run by independent farming families, and each has its own distinctive character. Choose the one that's nearest—or most interesting—to you by reviewing the following information.

Meadow Ridge Farm on the East Side offers hayrides at a $125 minimum, so you might want to get a group of friends together for this excursion, or see if the Smiths can fit you in with another group. But the planning is worth the effort. Meadow Ridge is set on 90 acres of rolling, wooded land. Linda and Art Smith have been at Meadow Ridge for more than 20 years, providing hayrides to newcomers and return customers every fall. "We have couples who meet on hayrides here and come back the following year as newlyweds," says Linda Smith.

The one-hour hayride at Meadow Ridge—pulled by a tractor,

not horses—takes you through rolling hills, woods, and open fields, and offers a view of the night sky, which Linda says is always beautiful in the fall. What you might enjoy most about the hayride is the simplicity of it. The absence of traffic noise, the stillness of the quiet country, the sounds of trees creaking and bending in the fall winds. One hour might not be long enough for this sentimental journey.

The end of your hayride is not the end of your evening. After the hayride you're invited to a bonfire at the Smiths'. You can cook out or enjoy some of the Huntsburg cider that is pressed nearby, and you're welcome to bring your own snacks. Enjoy the fireplace in the property's rustic lodge as you snuggle together against the freshly chilled night air.

On the south side of town Spring Mist Farms offers similar packages. Purists will like the fact that instead of tractors, the farm's equine employees—D.C., Topsy, Sassy, Bo, and Luke—pull the hay wagon. Dave Goodyear was raised on the farm and, with a laugh, describes his ride as "bumpy in parts, but mostly a nice ride that takes you through fields, woods, and a creek bed."

Typically, the rig will take you to the farm's lake—"The Lake of Spring Mist Farms," says Goodyear with an air of mystery in his voice—and drop you off there for an hour to enjoy a bonfire and snack on whatever it is you'd like to bring along. They'll pick you up after an hour or so and deliver you from the hayride to your car.

"My grandfather called this a farm that creates memories, and I guess that's true," says Goodyear, who has overseen a number of weddings on the property. He's even witnessed engagements from his perch at the helm of his hay wagon.

Both farms offer essentially the same thing: An evening that hearkens back to a more innocent time, when all that was needed for

Purists will like the fact that, instead of tractors, the farm's equine employees— D.C., Topsy, Sassy, Bo, and Luke— pull the hay wagon.

a romantic evening was a cart full of hay and friends to sit on top of it, telling stories, snuggling, and singing a song or two.

Variations:

Meadow Ridge and Spring Mist offer private hayrides, but there are additional spots that offer fall hayrides if you're willing to travel with strangers:

The Cleveland Metroparks also offer hayrides at various locations including the Chalet Recreation Area, the Mill Stream Run Reservation, and Swine Creek Reservation. These rides, more accessible to the general public, are a great way to meet new people—and require less planning on your part. Depending on where you go, you can expect storytelling, music, or even tours of "haunted forests" to accompany your ride. Call the Metroparks for more details; dates and times vary each season.

Directory

Cleveland Metroparks
4101 Fulton Pkwy. (Admin. Office), Cleveland
216-351-6300

HOURS/AVAILABILITY:
Call for times and locations.

Meadow Ridge Farm
17305 Mayfield Rd., Windsor
440-636-5420

HOURS/AVAILABILITY:
Call for reservation.

Spring Mist Farms
697 Pearl Rd., Brunswick
330-225-3565

HOURS/AVAILABILITY:
Call for reservation.

Outing 27
AN OLD-FASHIONED ICE-SKATING DAY

Season: Winter ~ **Time:** 3 hours
Location: West
Intimacy level: 1 ~ **Cost:** $–$$
Advance planning: none

What You'll Do

🠖 Shop for skates or have yours sharpened ($55 for new skates, under $10 for sharpening).

🠖 Skate doubles across a frozen pond.

🠖 Defy the cold by eating ice cream.

NOTE: *Lately our winters haven't been as cold as they used to be, creating a shortened outdoor ice-skating season. This outing takes you to Lakewood between the months of November and February, where you can skate outdoors, if the Lakewood Park rink is frozen, or indoors at nearby Winterhurst Municipal Ice Rink, if it's not.*

" *O*n skating over thin ice, our safety is in our speed." So said Ralph Waldo Emerson. In matters of love, as in skating, avoiding thin ice is the Golden Rule. Skating with someone you love or just happen to like an awful lot is a stimulating way to spend an afternoon or evening in the dead of winter. Of all sports, skating is most conducive to hand-holding. This kind of connection will help you to keep your balance—a valuable experiment in mutual trust.

Step by Step

2 P.M.: First, you'll need to get outfitted. The Skater's Edge carries a full line of ice skates, starting at around $55. You can pick up mittens, scarves, and hats as well as knee pads and other protective gear (highly recommended if you haven't been on the ice in a while). If you have an old pair of skates kicking around the house, have them sharpened here. (Though you can rent skates at Winterhurst—for use only at Winterhurst—there is no skate rental at Lakewood Park.)

3 P.M.: Throw those skates over your shoulder and head northward to Lakewood Park, a haven for would-be hockey stars and budding ice queens in the cold months of winter. If you've never skated outside before, you'll enjoy the challenge. The ice offers a bumpy ride—it requires a little more skill to navigate this tundra than an indoor rink. Once you get the hang of it, experience the thrill of gliding into Lake Erie's whipping wind, then turning around and letting it carry you to the south end of this frozen softball field. Support each other while you skate and offer a helping hand when your partner falls down. Take care on the ice—small sticks and frozen chunks of snow might get in your way.

4 P.M.: Defy the icicles by devouring them. After skating, go to Malley's Chocolates for a hot chocolate and—yes—ice cream. Malley's is a tradition in Lakewood year round. The pink-and-green interior features scenes from *Alice in Wonderland*. Boxes of chocolates, candies, and gift toys adorn the shopping area of the store, while the seating

Experience the thrill of gliding into
Lake Erie's whipping wind, then turning around
and letting the same wind carry you
to the south end of this frozen softball field.

area hosts sweet tooths who come in for a homemade sundae or a mug of cocoa. People think of Malley's as a summertime destination, but I say it's a great trip in winter. A dish of ice cream, a hot chocolate, and a few Malley's Billy Bobs—roasted pistachios wrapped in a blanket of caramel and covered with a thin layer of milk chocolate—are all foods that help store up necessary bulk for wintertime hibernation.

Variations:

INDOOR SKATING: Cleveland is home to a number of indoor ice arenas, most of which operate on a school-year schedule (it's very expensive to keep ice frozen in the middle of July) and charge admission fees that are generally under $5. Thornton Park Ice Rink is open year round, however, for those who feel the midsummer need for a skate. If you do find yourself at the rink during the summer, look around, you'll probably see some talented, dedicated skaters on the ice. Winterhurst Municipal Ice Rink is one of the largest rinks in the country. Because of its size, it is a part-time home for young, hopeful competitive skaters who work out there in the early hours of morning before school or go for a training skate in the evening.

At each rink you'll find the "regulars," couples who have been skating together for years. They glide across the ice with practiced skill. They are a testament to togetherness, these couples. You might even say that they've found a way to keep their relationship sharp.

Directory

Lakewood Park

Corner of Lake Ave. and Belle Ave., Lakewood

216-521-7580 (City Hall)

HOURS/AVAILABILITY:
Weather permitting, ice skating dawn–dusk during cold of winter.

Malley's Chocolates

14822 Madison Ave., Lakewood

216-529-6262

HOURS/AVAILABILITY:
Mon–Thu 10 a.m.–10 p.m., Fri–Sat 10 a.m.–midnight, Sun noon–10 p.m.

Skater's Edge

16211 Lorain Ave., Cleveland

216-252-3986

HOURS/AVAILABILITY:
Mon–Thu 10 a.m.–8 p.m., Tue and Fri 10 a.m.–9 p.m.

Thornton Park Ice Rink

20701 Farnsleigh Rd., Shaker Heights

216-491-1290

HOURS/AVAILABILITY:
Call for open skate times.

Winterhurst Municipal Ice Rink

14750 Lakewood Heights Blvd., Lakewood

216-529-4236

Hours/availability: Call for open skate times.

Outing 28
ANNIE, GET YOUR GUN

 Season: Any **Time:** 4 hours
Location: South ~ **Cost:** $–$$
Intimacy level: 2
Advance planning: None–Some

What You'll Do

🏹 Take a class in marksmanship or spend an afternoon in target practice.

🏹 Set your sights on some comfort food.

🏹 Catch an action flick.

*L*ove on the shooting range? It can happen. Adrienne Ross, producer at Channel 19 news, believes pistol packing is togetherness at its best. For some couples, it's a way to ensure safety, for others, it's just an entertaining way to pass time. For still others, target shooting is a healthy way to channel competitive energy. The pistol range can evoke the Wild West or simply give you a feeling of satisfaction and accomplishment. Try it out one afternoon for fun, and see if you and your love can hit the mark. Why not take a shot at it? Happiness, as the Beatles said, is a warm gun.

Step by Step

3 P.M.: The Stonewall Ltd. Gun Shop and Pistol Range is the place you want to shoot for. Most shooting ranges are private clubs that require

membership (they are geared toward servicing such organizations as the local police), but Stonewall is open to the public. In order to get right on the range, you must be an experienced gun owner or at least be accompanied by one. However, by completing a two-hour class in targeting, safety, and weapons use novices can qualify for target practice. The class is informative—and certainly a necessity for those not well versed in gunsmanship—offering practical advice on how to hold, load, and shoot a gun, and pointers on gun safety and self-defense.

When you get on the shooting range, develop your own system for healthy competition with your partner. Use the targets available to you, but turn them into your own game (such as pretending the targets are inanimate objects or aliens). Make friendly wagers—no gambling allowed!—making sure the loser buys dinner.

5 P.M.: When your ammo gives out, stop at the Courtyard for a bite to eat. According to Ross, they have "huge sandwiches and big ol' muffins" to fill you up after a hard day at the range. Take a seat in a cozy chair, order dinner, and enjoy the open-air atmosphere of this airy restaurant. Please check your guns at the door.

7 P.M.: Finish off your evening with an action-adventure movie at the Strongsville Cinemas. Watch with a new appreciation for technique—or critique the many safety infractions that will undoubtedly be committed throughout the course of the film.

Ross and her family spend time at the range at least a few times a month. "It's fun, it's a social place, and it's good for keeping in shape," says Ross.

Target shooting is a healthy way to channel competitive energy. The pistol range can evoke the Wild West or simply give you a feeling of satisfaction and accomplishment.

Variations:

SHOOTING WITHOUT THE BULLETS: You can have just as much fun shooting blanks, if you like, at the arcade. New and inventive video games can add an element of reality and 3-D to your shooting experience, and spending an afternoon in the arcade will definitely make you feel like a kid again. Besides, they don't give out furry stuffed animals at the shooting range. Power Play at the Power House has some of the most advanced shoot-em-up games in the city. When you tire of playing video games, make your way over to the Improv just across the hall for some rapid-fire comedy.

Directory

Courtyard Cafe
7600 Chippewa Rd., Brecksville
440-526-9292
HOURS/AVAILABILITY:
Mon–Thu 11 a.m.–10:30 p.m., Sat–Sun 11 a.m.-11:30 p.m.

Improv Comedy Club & Restaurant
2000 Sycamore St., Cleveland
216-696-4677
HOURS/AVAILABILITY:
Call for show times.

Power Play at the Power House
2000 Sycamore St., Cleveland
216-696-7664
HOURS/AVAILABILITY:
Mon–Thu noon–11 p.m., Fri–Sat noon–2 a.m., Sun closed

Stonewall Ltd. Gun Shop and Pistol Range
100 Ken-Mar Industrial Parkway, Broadview Hts.
440-526-0029
HOURS/AVAILABILITY:
Mon–Sat 7:30 a.m.–9:30 p.m., Sun 9 a.m.–7 p.m.

Strongsville Cinemas
14789 Pearl Rd., Strongsville
440-572-0134
HOURS/AVAILABILITY:
Call for movie times.

Outing 29

AUTUMN LEAVES: LET'S FALL IN LOVE

Season: Fall ~ **Time:** 2 hours, or overnight
Location: Far South
Intimacy level: 2–3 ~ **Cost:** $$–$$$
Advance Planning: Some–A lot

What You'll Do

❧ Take a country drive through the fall foliage.

❧ Rent a canoe on the Mohican River.

❧ Rest and relax at a Victorian inn.

NOTE: *When you drive the back roads of Ohio in the fall, a bounty of vistas and unexpected stops awaits you, as the fall colors on the trees signal that harvest season has arrived. Roadside stands dot these back roads as farmers sell homegrown apples, freshly pressed cider, and newly made apple butter. If you're a couple that likes to wander and take your time, reserve a spot at the Black Fork Inn a few weeks before you plan your fall foliage trip.*

Starting around the last week of September through the end of October, Ohio's trees put on a colorful show. While walks through your own neighborhood will provide evidence of these colors, you really can't feel the majesty of this phenomenon until you've had a breathtaking look at Ohio's rolling countryside. For a few short weeks, each tree displays a burst of color—some stand out through their own brilliance while others blend together to create a patchwork of colors that can make even Sherwin-Williams jealous. Share these memorable sights with someone you love on a long country drive one fall day.

Each year in Ohio is a bit different for the trees. The colors are dependent on factors that go way back to springtime—rainfall, sunshine, early frosts, and warm early fall days are factors that dictate what the fall colors will be like. The colors are tracked and checked throughout the season by the Ohio Department of Natural Resources. They maintain a Fall Foliage Report on the Web at www.dnr.state.oh.us-odnr-color-. The website provides photos that are updated almost daily, as well as educational information about where the colors come from and printable maps of routes you can take to find the best foliage sites. Those without Web access can call 800-BUCKEYE for daily reports.

Bill Schultz, information officer for the Ohio Division of Forestry at the Department of Natural Resources, describes himself as a frustrated photographer. He and his wife love to go out hiking, and taking pictures throughout the year, but Schultz admits that fall is his favorite time for photographs and nature walks. He recommends taking trails that are near waterways. "On a still day, the water in some of our lakes can get as flat as glass, and it amplifies—actually doubles—the colors you'll see."

Step by Step

2 P.M.: Mohican State Park is one of the best places to see the display. You can hike, canoe, or just drive around Mohican for an afternoon, surrounded by color and earthy fall smells. Schultz puts the park in his list of top three areas of the state for fall colors; the other two are the

The colors are dependent on factors that go way back to springtime: rainfall, sunshine, early frosts, and warm early fall days are factors that dictate what the fall colors will be like.

Hocking Hills in the southern part of the state and a stretch of I-71 just north of Columbus.

Though the easiest way to get to Mohican is via I-71, you'll want to meander through country roads to get there. Plan to leave the house early on a bright fall day, taking a route that is off the beaten path. My favorite route from Cleveland is to take I-71 south to SR83. Take 83 into Wooster. Once you are past Wooster, make your way to Mohican State Park via SR95. You'll find plenty to do at the park. Long trails and footpaths follow the Mohican River, but the main attraction here is the Mohican Canoe Livery and Fun Center. Rent a canoe or kayak and take a leisurely two-hour run along the river, just the two of you, and take in the sights of fall.

5 P.M.: In Loudonville you'll find the Black Fork Inn, owned by Sue and Al Gorisek. Built in the late 1800s, this is the kind of place people might connect with ghost stories, but don't worry, the only spirits here are contained in cocktail glasses.

"Taking someone you love a bouquet of colorful leaves may be just as romantic as taking a dozen roses."

Sue Gorisek is the quintessential innkeeper. You'll likely come across her in the front yard working in the garden, where she'll breezily greet you and welcome you with an outstretched, garden-gloved hand. Upon entering the inn, you'll see the fruits of her labors, as the parlor and the front desk are generally strewn with freshly cut flowers from her garden.

The rooms at the Black Fork maintain this Victorian theme, but are also modern and cozy. Downtown Loudonville is only a few blocks down the street, and you can find little shops, a movie house, and plenty of friendly townspeople to talk with.

The next day over breakfast be sure to ask Gorisek for some leads on where the best fall colors are. She has a home in Cleveland and has traveled every road between Cleveland and Loudonville at least twice in her old truck.

Before you leave the Mansfield area, visit the Richland Carousel Park for a ride on a vintage carousel. This unassuming town is also the place where Bogie and Bacall were married at Malabar Farm, a manor house owned at the time by Louis Bromfield, a novelist and playwright. The farm is now a historic site open to the public.

I-71 is the most direct route home, but pay close attention to roadside attractions along the way and make the best of these fall days. The countryside is beautiful, so take one last walk along a country road if you can squeeze it in. Bill Schultz suggests that you pick up a bouquet of leaves from the ground: "I think taking some-one you love a bouquet of colorful leaves may be just as romantic as taking them a dozen roses. That would make a nice presentation in this part of the year."

Variations:

CORNY, BUT FUN: If you want to make a keepsake of your day, reach back into early childhood when Mom would preserve leaves for you in wax paper. The technology hasn't changed much, and you can still make a keepsake leaf bookmark in short order. For a bookmark, find a leaf or two that are long, thin, and full of color. Take them home and bust out the waxed paper you keep in the drawer. Arrange the leaves as you'd like them while heating up your iron. Now all you need to do is iron over the waxed paper and leaves, and you have a lovely memento with which to keep your place.

Directory

Black Fork Inn
303 North Water St.,
Loudonville
419-994-3252
HOURS/AVAILABILITY:
Call for reservation.

Malabar Farm State Park
4050 Bromfield Rd., Lucas
419-892-2784
HOURS/AVAILABILITY:
Varies, please call ahead.

Mohican Canoe Livery & Fun Center
3045 SR 3, Loudonville
419-994-4020
HOURS/AVAILABILITY:
April 1–October 31
9 a.m.–9 p.m.

Mohican State Park
3116 SR. 3, Loudonville
800-282-7275
HOURS/AVAILABILITY:
Daily dawn–dusk

Richland Carousel Park
75 N. Main St., Mansfield
419 522 4223
HOURS/AVAILABILITY:
Daily 11 a.m.–5 p.m.,
Wed 11 a.m.–8 p.m.

Outing 30

A WRINKLE IN TIME

Season: Any ~ **Time:** 12 hours
Location: West
Intimacy level: 1 ~ **Cost:** $$
Advance planning: Some

What You'll Do

🔹 Tour the future at NASA Glenn Visitor's Center.

🔹 Watch the present fly by from the airport observation deck.

🔹 Dine amidst WWII aviation memorabilia ($25–$40).

From the time Icarus took his ill-fated flight, mankind dreamt of mastering the skies—until two brothers from Ohio finally achieved liftoff with their amazing flying machine. Sure, there were hot air balloons, but airplanes gave us control in the skies. Their propulsion engines meant we would no longer be entirely dependent on winds and weather. In the span of less than a century, we've pushed the boundaries of our frontier onward to space. In the span of one evening in Cleveland, you can see first hand how space travel is made possible by the brain trust at NASA, view giant jets as they whoosh by only a few hundred feet from your head, and sample the romantic early days of early flight.

Step by Step

ANY AFTERNOON, 3 P.M.: The NASA Glenn Visitor's Center opens its doors during the week, offering visitors an opportunity to view the lab. Its educational exhibits—designed mainly for children and young adults—are just as intriguing to adults who tour them. The Apollo Skylab 3 capsule is a study in claustrophobia, the sight of which will give you a new appreciation for the technology of space travel. But on this particular tour, you will also be able to see the NASA test facilities. The tour takes about an hour.

4:30 P.M.: For an after-tour snack, grab a self-indulgent cinnamon bun or cookie that you'll pick up on the way to the airport observation deck at Hopkins. Located in Concourse B—and decidedly in the present—on the third floor, the observation deck is a peaceful oasis amidst the flurry of activity above and below you. The deck overlooks the airfield and runways, and on clear afternoons you can see farther east for a view of the city. Relax and enjoy your sweet snack while planes land and take off. Apply the theories you learned at NASA to the marvel of air flight. Seeing the size and girth of the large jets as they taxi through the runway system, it becomes mind-boggling to think that such a massive amount of steel, more than 100 people, and all of their heavy luggage can be so gracefully delivered into the sky. This is usually a good moment for a kiss—especially if the deck is not crowded with travelers. Take advantage of it, and do a little soaring of your own.

6 P.M.: Go back in time by traveling a few blocks to the One Hundredth Bomb Group restaurant. As you enter the grounds, notice the landscaping. Jeeps, an army supply truck, and even a vintage speaker system adorn the front lawn, turning this small strip of Brookpark Road into a European town circa 1942. Inside, big band music plays

Jeeps, and army supply truck, and even a vintage speaker system adorn the front lawn, turning this small strip of Brookpark Road into a European town circa 1942.

amidst relics from the war era. But the food isn't rationed. In fact, you'll be served heaps of real potatoes, thick juicy steaks, and seafood fresh off a daily flight from the East Coast. Enjoy the atmosphere and the view—the glass frontage ensures clear sight of planes taking off and landing at the airport just across the way.

Variations:

BUILD YOUR OWN PLANE: At Wings Hobby Shop, flight is fancy. Model plane kits—from the simplest to the most complex—represent every era and almost every kind of flight. But the coolest of the cool planes are the remote-controlled ones that actually fly! Such planes are available as kits or already assembled. Once you've purchased the plane, spend the afternoon at Memorial field in the nearby Rocky River Reservation—the big, open space and total absence of power lines will give you plenty of room to play with your new toy.

Directory

Cleveland Hopkins International Airport Observation Deck

5300 Riverside Dr., Cleveland

216-265-6030

HOURS/AVAILABILITY:
Daily 10 a.m.–10 p.m.

NASA Glenn Research Center Visitor Center

2100 Brookpark Rd., Berea

216-433-2001

HOURS/AVAILABILITY:
Open for tours Mon–Fri 9 a.m.–4 p.m., Sat 10 a.m.–3 p.m., Sun 1 p.m.–5 p.m.; or call 433-2000 to register for Wed 2 p.m. or third Saturday at 1 p.m. programs.

One Hundredth Bomb Group

20000 Brookpark Rd., Cleveland

216-267-1010

HOURS/AVAILABILITY:
Mon–Fri 11 a.m.–3 p.m. and 4:30 p.m.–11 p.m., Sat 11 a.m.–2:30 p.m. and 4:30 p.m.–11 p.m., Sun 9:30 a.m.–2:30 p.m. (brunch) and 4:30 p.m.–10 p.m.

Rocky River Reservation

24000 Valley Pkwy., North Olmsted

216-351-6300

HOURS/AVAILABILITY:
Daily dawn–dusk

Wings Hobby Shop

17112 Detroit Rd., Lakewood

216-221-5383

HOURS/AVAILABILITY:
Mon and Fri 10 a.m.–8 p.m., Tue and Thu 10 a.m.–6 p.m., Wed and Sat 10 a.m.–5:30 p.m., Sun 12:30 p.m.–5 p.m.

Outing 31

ROMANCE IS BREWING

Season: All ~ **Time:** 4–6 hours
Location: Near West
Intimacy level: 1 ~ **Cost:** $$
Advance planning: None

What You'll Do

➤ Tour a working brewery ($3).

➤ Enjoy a glass of ale or stout with lunch ($20–$35).

➤ Embark on a comparison tour ($30–$40).

*T*here is a story in my family about our Uncle Gibbers and the German brewer. Apparently in the early 1900s my grandfather, a contractor, had a large number of horses and wagons that weren't in use during the day, and the German brewer in town had need of horses and wagons to deliver his kegs of beer. Grandpa factored his brother, Gibbers, into the equation as a salesperson, and it seemed like a foolproof deal for everyone involved. The only problem was that Gibbers would take beer orders from the pub but, being a polite Irishman, couldn't leave without buying a round for himself and a few of the friends who were invariably there with him (indeed, any fella drinking stout in a pub was a friend of Gibbers's). This ritual would go on until midafternoon every day, at which point my grandfather would send out some of his workers to "find Gibbers and get him back here before he drinks all the money."

Needless to say, Gibbers didn't last long as the beer salesman. But I still wonder if the brewer in question was Mr. Schlather, who owned the brewery that is now operated by the Great Lakes Brewing Company. Even now, I imagine the ghost of Gibbers enjoying a pint of stout at the company's beautiful bar with not a care in the world.

But you needn't be a sentimentalist to recognize the romance brewing at Great Lakes. The Conway family (who own the place) have built up their business from a small microbrewery to an award-winning brewery and major tourist attraction in the space of only a few years. In doing so, they've realized the American Dream: produce a high-quality product, add some sweat equity, and you'll find success. A walk through this restaurant and its new brewing facility just across the street is more than just an education in how beer is made. It's a lesson in the importance of following your dreams to fruition as the Conways have and maintaining your high standards for quality along the way.

Step by Step

11:30 A.M.: Sign up for a tour at the main reception desk of the Great Lakes Brewing Company. As you wait for the tour to begin, sit at the bar and ask to see the famed bullet holes in the back-bar. It is said—and many variations of the story exist—that Elliot Ness used to drink here, and that shots from his own gun are responsible for these holes. Before the building became a bar, it was a feed store. Another notable entrepreneur once worked in this space: the store had among its employees an enterprising young John D. Rockefeller, whose bookkeeping desk is on display at Great Lakes.

The tour begins in the cellar, where the fermenting tanks hold thousands of gallons of beer, ale, and lager at various stages of the brewing process. Until 1998, this series of cramped rooms was

Ask to see the famed bullet holes in the back-bar.
It is said that Eliot Ness used to drink here,
and that the shots from his own gun
are responsible for these holes.

where all of the Great Lakes Brewing Company's beer was brewed. Then the Conways purchased the Volunteers of America building and invested $7 million, expanding their operation from a 7-barrel microbrewery to a 75-barrel powerhouse, and making Great Lakes the largest brewer in town.

As you walking over to the new building, the guide provides bits and pieces of neighborhood history along with the details of how beer is made, what ingredients make up a good batch of beer, and how different styles of beer are brewed. Because Great Lakes is a true local brewery, the beer does not go through a pasteurization process that would give it a longer shelf life. Instead, the brewer gauges his market and produces just enough beer to last through the natural shelf life of each bottle.

In the new facility, giant vats of beer are regulated by gauges that provide temperature and pressure readings. The technical side of beer brewing is described as the sounds and smells of brewing surround you. Home brewers are particularly interested in this aspect of brewing, asking questions about timing, the best way to mix ingredients, and various techniques for achieving the highest-quality beers.

Home beer drinkers will enjoy the final phase of the tour, in which the group returns to the restaurant for a glass of ale.

1 P.M.: After the tour, indulge in a lunch at the brewery—if the weather permits ask for a seat in the lovely outdoor beer garden. Choose a beer-filled meal: beer-cheese soup, followed by beer-battered fish and chips. At present, there seem to be no beer desserts, but give them time, I'm sure they'll invent something.

2:30 P.M.: Though Great Lakes is the first and the biggest, it's not the only brewery in town. Make an afternoon of taste-testing local beers, being mindful, of course, of the amount of beer you consume if you're driving. Downtown Cleveland is home to the Rock Bottom Brewery. Stop in, take a look at their brewing equipment, and sample their beers, comparing the flavor of each with that of the last.

Microbrewed beers are often fleeting. They'll mix a batch up for one season, then move on to a new recipe for the next. Stay on your toes with each passing season by stopping in regularly to try the new brews, loudly voicing your opinions on the ones you like best— they'll bring back the more popular brews over time.

Variations:

EXPERIMENT WITH YOUR OWN MICROBREWERY: Home brewing beer together
can be a simple process, if you know what you're doing and follow
the rules. Brewing supplies are available at Warehouse Brewing Supplies, where an investment of about $100 will buy you a brewing kit,
bottles, and all the ingredients needed for setting up a home brewery. Don't get frustrated if the brewing process goes awry . . . help is
available through SNOB (the Society of Northeast Ohio Brewers).
On the first Monday of every month, from 7 p.m. to 9 p.m. this well-
organized, dedicated group of brewers meets at the Great Lakes
Brewing Company to discuss home brewing. This helpful group of
people can give advice on technique, recipes, and even bottling. Join
them for an evening of networking, and a sip or two.

Directory

**Great Lakes
Brewing Company**

2516 Market Ave., Cleveland

216-771-4404

HOURS/AVAILABILITY:
Mon–Thu 11:30 a.m.–
10:30 p.m. (bar until
midnight), Fri and Sat
11:30 a.m.–11:30 p.m.
(bar until 1 a.m.),
Sun 3 p.m.–9 p.m.

**Rock Bottom
Brewing Company**

2000 Sycamore St., Cleveland

216-623-1555

HOURS/AVAILABILITY:
Mon–Sat 11:30 a.m.–2 a.m.,
Sun 11:30 p.m.–10 a.m.
(bar until 1 a.m.)

**Warehouse Brewing
Supplies**

4364 Mayfield, South Euclid

216-382-2400

HOURS/AVAILABILITY:
Mon–Fri 9 a.m.–10 p.m.,
Sat–Sun 9:30 a.m.–10 p.m.

Outing 32

THE BRIDGES OF ASHTABULA COUNTY

Season: Any ~ **Time:** 6–8 hours
Location: Farther East
Intimacy level: 1 ~ **Cost:** $–$$
Advance planning: None–Some

What You'll Do

🏹 Take a covered bridge driving tour in Ashtabula County.

🏹 Break for lunch at a roadside restaurant ($15–$30).

🏹 In warm weather, take a plunge in a swimming hole.

NOTE: *Call the Ashtabula County Convention and Visitor's Bureau before you go to request a driving tour map and guide that will help you navigate this country landscape and provide information on each of the bridges you'll see.*

Covered bridges are part of the romance of early America. Such bridges are often the subject of paintings that portray the charm and details of life in New England in the 1700s and 1800s. The bridges were originally built to be practical—not picturesque. Covering stone bridges kept them from freezing over in the winter months. With a roof to shield them from the rain and side walls to break the fall of a skidding carriage, these bridges served their purpose well until modern inventions like guardrails could take their place. Many of these covered bridges met their end at the beginning of this century. They either were washed out and never rebuilt or fell into such disrepair that they had to be torn down. But in Ashtabula County covered bridges are maintained and revered, providing visitors with an accurate glimpse into the romantic days of yore when a covered bridge was both charming and functional.

Touring the bridges will take you through country roads and beautiful scenery. Take time to walk along the pathways, and get out of the car to really observe the construction of the bridges. There are picnic areas and restaurants along the way, so plan to spend the day immersed in this countryside exploration together.

Before you go, call the Ashtabula County Convention and Visitor's Bureau to request a guide and map.

Ashtabula County bridges, maintained and revered, provide a glimpse into the romantic days of yore.

Step by Step

10 A.M.: In Jefferson, you'll begin a journey through 11 covered bridges. Following are highlights of the tour, along with a suggestion for lunch:

NETCHER ROAD BRIDGE: This new bridge spans Mill Creek. Construction should be completed in 1999, revealing a historically accurate Victorian design.

SOUTH DENMARK ROAD BRIDGE: A vintage structure, built in 1890, this bridge is complemented by a more modern bridge to lighten the traffic load.

CAINE ROAD COVERED BRIDGE: Constructed in honor of Ashtabula County's 175th anniversary, this bridge makes use of modern construction techniques. It is 96 feet long and is a rare example of "old replacing new," as this covered bridge was built over a more modern steel truss bridge.

GRAHM ROAD BRIDGE: This bridge was washed away in the flood of 1913, but residents collected the remnants and rebuilt the bridge, which now sits in a small park on the south side of the road. A grill adorns the steps that lead up to the bridge's interior, with a picnic table just inside the bridge itself. Walking through this bridge will give you the safest tour of the interior of a covered bridge, as the only traffic that can charge through is pedestrian.

ROOT ROAD BRIDGE: This bridge got a lift in 1982 when it was raised 18 inches to accommodate the changing landscape. Originally built in 1868, the bridge is now supported with laminated girders and a center concrete pier.

MIDDLE ROAD BRIDGE: This bridge dates back to 1868 and spans Conneaut Creek. When it was originally built, the bridge boasted a new "X" design that would allow it to be adjusted whenever it began to sag. The idea took off, and hundreds of bridges around the country employed this new, functional design. In 1984 volunteers reconstructed the bridge, restoring its original splendor.

NOON: LUNCH AT THE BEEF AND BEER: The name says it all. Stop in this roadside restaurant for a family-style meal in a country atmosphere. Steaks are freshly cut on the premises, and chicken or fish dinners are served in hearty portions. Fuel up with a big meal for the return ride through the countryside.

STATE ROAD BRIDGE: Some 97,000 feet of southern pine and oak were used in the construction of this bridge in 1983. The bridge also has a window that spans its length, giving travelers an uncommon view from inside. The dedication ceremony for the bridge sparked Ashtabula's annual covered bridge festival.

CREEK ROAD BRIDGE: Well over 100 years old, this bridge is known for its height—raised 25 feet above Conneaut Creek.

BENETKA ROAD BRIDGE: This bridge was built in 1900 and is thought to be one of the most attractive bridges on the tour. Fully renovated, it paints a lovely picture. Take some time to walk around the area and view it from afar.

The bridge now sits in a small park on the south side of the road. A grill adorns the steps that lead up to the bridge's interior, with a picnic table just inside the bridge itself.

3 P.M.: If weather permits, take a swim at the Olin Bridge. This bridge was built on property owned by the Olin family in 1873. Just to the west of the bridge, you'll find the Ashtabula River swimming hole. Take a dip, if you like, the tour is almost finished.

GIDDINGS ROAD BRIDGE: This final bridge is yet another example of new construction. Built with state funding, the bridge is 107 feet long. Crossing Mill Creek, it leads you back into Jefferson Township, concluding your tour.

Directory

Ashtabula County Convention & Visitor's Bureau

1850 Austinburg Rd., Ashtabula

800-337-6746

HOURS/AVAILABILITY:
Office: Mon–Fri
8:30 a.m.–5:30 p.m.

Beef and Beer

57 Underridge Rd., Conneaut

440-593-3667

HOURS/AVAILABILITY:
Sun–Thu 11 a.m.–8 p.m.,
Fri–Sat 11 a.m.–9 p.m.

Outing 33
WINERIES

Season: All ~ **Time:** 4 hours
Location: West
Intimacy level: 1 ~ **Cost:** $$–$$$
Advance planning: None

What You'll Do

🏹 Take a winery tour and sip on the fruits of the vintner's labor.

🏹 Lunch at a villa ($25–$40).

🏹 Shop for fresh Ohio grapes, then make your own wine ($3–$30).

When man first decided to alter his lifestyle from nomadic to agrarian, one of his top priorities was fermentation. Winemaking has been a mainstay and an art form ever since. The process is amazingly simple: mix crushed grapes with sugar and water and wait. But refining the process to make wines that appeal appropriately to the senses can take years. And so wine has about it a mystique, a captivating romance that draws us to it and drinks us in. When visiting a winery, first you notice the smell—wood moistened by aging wine, combined with the aroma of fresh, new grapes and a variety of spices that cling to the air. Walking through the process together is a lesson in history—and in love. The winemaker's ancient task is one of patience and commitment as he waits—sometimes years—for his wine to ferment, age, and mature. At the end of the tour, visitors are rewarded with a product of the winemaker's toil, and with a new metaphor to apply to the maturation of their own relationship.

Step by Step

NOON: Tour a winery. One of the last remaining wineries in this area is the Heartland Vineyards. The winery, in operation since 1934, was once the largest supplier and shipper of wine in Ohio. Now, it produces just under 50,000 gallons of wine each year in its charming facility.

"There's a lot of history here," says winery owner Jerome Welliver, who has owned the business since 1998. "Until about 1816, Ohio was the place for wine production. Then in the 1900s, this winery was a top producer," says Welliver. Throughout the winery, walls are adorned with photographs and illustrations depicting wine production and the men and women who worked here over the years.

On the tour, you'll walk through the wine-producing process, first learning about the tools of the trade; grape crushing, mixing, bottling, corking, and labeling are all discussed. Next, walk into the winery area, which includes tanks that take up the full length of the room as well as cold storage tanks, some holding as many as 6,000 gallons of wine in different stages of production. Join in the discussion about the length of time required for the aging process, aging techniques, and the testing of the maturing process, asking questions along the way. The bottling and corking area is also housed here, providing an opportunity for some hands-on experience corking a bottle.

Finally, guests are invited into the wine-tasting room, located in the cellar of the building. It has the feel of a wine cellar: dark wood, stone, and empty wine barrels adorn this space where guests are invited to take a few sips of the winery's finest products.

It has the feel of a wine cellar:
dark wood, stone, and empty wine barrels
adorn this space where guests are invited
to take a few sips of the winery's finest products.

Sit back, sip wine, and get a useful education on the basics of wine—the varieties available, how to tell good wine from bad, and what to look for on the label and in the bottle. Munch on cheeses and bread to cleanse the palate, move on to the next taste test, and get to know the likes and dislikes of your partner. Debating wine and its qualities can become a lifelong passion for the two of you.

1 P.M.: After the tour, it's a short walk up a flight of stairs to Mahle's, a small, snug restaurant that serves classic American fare with a twist of Italian. Owner Beverly Mahle works with the winery downstairs to produce the restaurant's distinctive brand of wine. At Mahle's you can munch on sandwiches or pasta entrees.

2:30 P.M.: If the trip to the winery inspires you to make some wine of your own, pick up some supplies on your way out. Heartland sells equipment needed for wine-making, including bottled, crushed grapes to save you the hassle of having to crush the grapes yourself.

Directory

Heartland Vineyards
24945 Detroit Rd., Westlake
440-871-0700
HOURS/AVAILABILITY:
Tue–Sat noon–6 p.m.

Mahle's
24945 Detroit Rd., Westlake
440-899-6602
HOURS/AVAILABILITY:
Mon–Thu 11 a.m.–9 p.m.,
Fri –Sat 11 a.m.–10 p.m.,
Sun closed

Outing 34
DOING THE DRIVE-IN

Season: Spring, Summer, Fall
Time: 3–4 hours ~ **Location:** South
Intimacy level: 1 ~ **Cost:** $–$$
Advance Planning: Some

What You'll Do

- Rent a wreck to enhance your viewing experience.
- Pack the car with blankets and goodies.
- Take in a flick at the Memphis Drive-In.

> **NOTE:** *Among the more important ingredients to a successful night at the drive-in movies is a car with bench seating. If your car doesn't fit the bill, you'll need to borrow, or rent one. You'll also want to put together a few items to take along including a blanket and battery-powered radio for tuning in to the film (make sure you've got fresh batteries), a few pillows, and maybe some home-popped popcorn.*

There are wrong ways and right ways to do certain things, and when you're involved in that particularly American ritual of going to the drive-in movie, you need to do it right. Whether you're newly dating or a veteran couple, you can't help but feel like a teenager when you pull your car into just the right space and snuggle up in the front seat for an evening of watching movies through your windshield.

Step by Step

THREE DAYS BEFORE THE DATE: Rent a car with bench seats. If you have a friend who has an older-model car you can borrow, all the better. Once you explain why you need the bench seats, he'll understand. If you have no such friends, call ahead of time to reserve such a car with Rent-A-Wreck in Parma. For less than $20 a day, you can buy yourself an evening of closeness. They still have a few cars in rotation that will meet your needs, but you'll want to make sure you've specified your order in time.

5:00 P.M.: Get the car. There are really only three key ingredients to enjoying a drive-in experience. A date, some popcorn, and a car with bench seats. You remember bench seats, don't you? The front seat of the car was designed to be one long bench so that there was nothing like a gearshift to interrupt the space between you and your snuggly date. These days, cars are designed with two very separate bucket seats, often with a shift right in the middle—convenient for operating a car, but very uncomfortable for steering your date closer to you.

8:00 P.M.: Check the drive-in schedule ahead of time. Drive-in movie schedules generally follow sunset times—which are a little later in July than in, say, September. But generally, the flicks won't start until about 9:00. Before you leave the house, pack a few items that will help make your evening more pleasant. You'll want a radio stocked with fresh batteries in order to receive a broadcast of the movie's sound, a warm blanket to ward off the evening chill, and a few pillows to help you create a more comfortable environment in the front seat of the car—or back seat. That's up to you.

There are really only three key ingredients
to enjoying a drive-in experience: A date,
some popcorn, and a car with bench seats.

Though half the fun of going to the drive-in is eating the concession stand fare of hot dogs, popcorn, candy, and pop, some connoisseurs (like me) insist on bringing a stash of candy and home-popped popcorn. Popcorn is a key ingredient to any good movie, so if you're popping at home, make sure you have a covered container to store it in (you don't want to spill popcorn all over the car while you're driving). Take melted butter in a Thermos for use at the drive-in, and bring along a small shaker of popcorn salt, too.

9:00 P.M.: I like the Memphis Drive-In for a few reasons. First of all, I like the name. Not understanding geography when I was young, I always thought we were going deep into country-and-western land when we pulled into Memphis. The big lot that is the Memphis Drive-In seems to have its very own brand of unintentional kitsch—it's dingy, but in a way that is heartwarming instead of annoying. It might be just a parking lot and a screen, but on summer nights you can't see the cracks in the pavement or the rust on the girders that support the screen—you just see stars in the sky and on the colorful screen.

The Memphis Drive-In has three screens, offering on any given night a smattering of horror movies, chick flicks, slasher films, and

westerns. Take your pick of films, then get your pick of spaces by arriving at least fifteen minutes early. This will give you time—if you like—to get a fresh soda at the concession stand and settle in to watch movies.

The Memphis Drive-In has three screens, offering on any given night a smattering of horror movies, chick flicks, slasher films, and westerns.

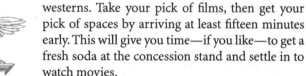
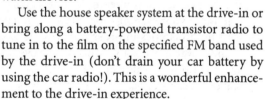

Use the house speaker system at the drive-in or bring along a battery-powered transistor radio to tune in to the film on the specified FM band used by the drive-in (don't drain your car battery by using the car radio!). This is a wonderful enhancement to the drive-in experience.

Ardent film fans might want to block out the rest of the world by bringing earphones and walkmans, but I think that dilutes the charm of the drive-in experience. Why block out the sound of couples smooching, or kids fighting over the last Raisinette? That's Americana at its best.

Sometime during the first half of the movie, snuggle close and take advantage of this publicly intimate setting. Unlike a regular movie theater, the drive-in offers you an opportunity to enjoy all the benefits of the big screen and the intimacy of home in one place.

There is another secret to the drive-in experience I think helps reaffirm that there really is romance in the world. Midway through the film—if you can tear yourself away from the plot and your honey—take a slow walk to the concession stand. As you walk through the lot, practice a little voyeurism. You'll see couples kissing, holding hands, and snuggling in almost every car. Parents will steal a glance to the back seat to see if the kids are asleep yet, and steal a kiss before returning their gaze to the screen. You might even catch a young couple having their first "car date kiss."

AFTER MIDNIGHT: When the movie is over, throw away the candy wrappers and discarded popcorn kernels—but don't fold the blankets up quite yet. I suggest that you take one last opportunity in this car of yours to pretend you're still in high school. Make believe it's your first date, and take advantage of your bench seats to make out in the parking lot. Make out until the car windows fog up, then make out some more. Youth isn't just for the young, you know.

Directory

Memphis Drive-In
10543 Memphis Ave., Cleveland
216-941-2892
HOURS/AVAILABILITY:
Summer Mon—Sat
8 p.m.–1 a.m.

Rent-A-Wreck
8003 Brookpark Rd., Parma
216/351/1840
HOURS/AVAILABILITY:
Mon—Fri 8 a.m.–6 p.m.,
Sat 9 a.m.–1 p.m.

138

Outing 35
HIS NIGHT OUT

Season: Any ~ **Time:** 6–8 hours
Location: Downtown, Near West
Intimacy level: 1–3 ~ **Cost:** $$$–$$$$
Advance planning: Some

What You'll Do

- Chomp on thick steaks downtown ($50–$100).
- Shout at the refs at the ballgame of his choice ($60–$300).
- Smoke cigars and shoot stick at a neighborhood joint ($20–$30).

NOTE: *A few weeks (at least) before you go: Get tickets to the game. The best seats you can find. Whatever game it is he likes. Pull strings with friends who have season tickets or call a ticket broker, but be sure you get good seats.*

My Aunt Dee and Uncle Terry are one of the best-suited couples I know. Married for at least 40 years, they will happily tell you that they're still madly in love. But behind his back, my Aunt Dee will say: "You like your Uncle Terry? Yeah, well he wasn't so great when I met him." Aunt Dee believes that relationships are hard work for both parties, and only a healthy mix of perseverance, patience, and indulgence will result in the outcome she's been lucky enough to achieve: a happy life together. Every so often, Dee indulges her husband with a night something like the one described below, a night designed just for him. It might be a ballgame, or an evening of classical music—Terry is fanatical about the Cleveland Orchestra—but it is designed specifically for him because, as Aunt Dee says, "Every once in a while you have to give them time off for good behavior."

The goal is to plan an evening that he'll enjoy. This can be as simple as staying in and enthusiastically watching the game, or it can be as elaborate as an evening on the town done his way. The following is a recipe for romance whose key ingredients are meat and potatoes and a ballgame.

Step by Step

6 P.M.: Have dinner at Morton's, complete with steaks, cigars, and martinis. The dark paneling on the walls combined with the heavy cloud of cigar smoke about the place gives off the feeling of a private men's club in New York. But it's also a place for serious eating. The steaks really are worth the trip, the swordfish is grilled beautifully, and potatoes are cooked with every ounce of respect due to the spud, resulting in crispy, brown home fries.

The heavy cloud of cigar smoke about the place gives off the feeling of a private men's club in New York.

7:30 P.M.: Go to the game with lots of cash in your pocket. Games are expensive—from parking to beverages to ball caps, you can drop a hefty sum at the Jake or the Gund. The game will be the centerpiece of his conversation for weeks to come, though, so it's worth the expense. Enjoy yourself, let loose, yell, buy peanuts, agree with the people sitting next to you. During the game, make sure to purchase a ball cap or other souvenir for him to show off to his buddies.

10:30 P.M.: After dinner, stop at the Fulton Bar and Grill. Designed, owned, and operated by two of Cleveland's most raffish bachelors, the Fulton is a gentleman's club in its own right. A mural features a bar crowd from the 1920s or '30s enjoying themselves. The bar is fully stocked with macho drinks—single malt Scotch, Irish whiskeys, cognacs. Cozy lounge chairs add to the gaming-room atmosphere upstairs at the Fulton, while the warm fires of the kitchen act as a sort of makeshift fireplace for the room.

Let him bask in the evening, and never utter the words, "are you getting tired?" Most importantly, let him feel like he's running things. After an evening like the one described above, Aunt Dee would shrug, "Eh, you gotta keep 'em happy. C'mon Terry, let's go."

Variations:

MAN CANNOT LIVE ON SPORTS ALONE: Though they may not admit to it all the time, men like getting a new suit. It's getting them to shop for the new suit that could be the problem. Make an appointment at the Armani section at Saks Fifth Avenue to have him fitted. This luxury will ensure him a good fit, a new suit, and a great look. Plan to spend the better portion of an afternoon for the first fitting, looking through patterns and fabric styles, getting measured, and ordering a new suit. There will probably be a need to return for an additional fitting at least once, but don't worry—men like the preening and the attention a lot more than they'll admit. He'll be particularly happy if you're buying, Sadie Hawkins. Giovanni's is the logical stop for dinner. Here you can have first-rate service while you put an extra inch on your waistlines eating gourmet pastas and sauces, steaks, and desserts.

Directory

Cleveland Cavaliers
One Center Court, Cleveland
216-420-2000
HOURS/AVAILABILITY:
Call for game times.

Fulton Bar and Grill
1835 Fulton Rd., Cleveland
216-694-2122
HOURS/AVAILABILITY:
Mon–Fri 4:30 p.m.–2:30 a.m.,
Sat–Sun 6 p.m.–2:30 a.m.;
Weekend reservations
necessary.

Morton's
1600 W. 2nd St., Cleveland
216-621-6200
HOURS/AVAILABILITY:
Mon–Sat 5:30 p.m.–11:00
p.m., Sun 5 p.m.–10 p.m.

Ristorante Giovanni's
25550 Chagrin Blvd., Beachwood
216-831-8625
HOURS/AVAILABILITY:
Mon–Fri noon–2:30 p.m.
and 5:30 p.m.–10 p.m., Sat
5 p.m.–10:30 p.m., closed Sun

Saks Fifth Ave.
26100 Cedar Rd., Beachwood
216-292-5500
HOURS/AVAILABILITY:
Mon–Fri 10 a.m.–9 p.m.,
Sat 10 a.m.–7:30 p.m.,
Sun noon–6 p.m.

Outing 36
ROMANCE ON THE HOG

Season: Any ~ **Time:** 2 hours
Location: South
Intimacy level: 1 ~ **Cost:** $
Advance planning: None

What You'll Do

🡒 Visit Biker's Mecca right here in Northeast Ohio.

🡒 Taste Cleveland's heartiest burger.

🡒 Take a two-wheeled test drive.

*D*espite the respectability heaped on this pastime recently by such upscale spokesmen as Jay Leno, motorcycling just can't shake the James Dean image. And maybe it shouldn't. It takes a certain amount of guts to climb aboard one of these machines, then careen through traffic at high speeds protected only by your skill as a driver. But damn it's fun. Ohioans seem to think so—Ohio's motorcycle population is the second-largest in the country.

A number of elements contribute to the romance of the motorcycle. Certainly the bad-boy image projected by James Dean in the 1950s is chief among them. And Hunter S. Thompson's book *Hell's Angels: A Strange and Terrible Saga* paints a colorful portrait of a band of motorcycle outlaws who roamed San Francisco in the '60s and '70s. But when it comes right down to it, motorcycles are the modern answer to the horse and saddle. Just looking at a motorcycle can conjure up images of getting away and exploring America, just you, your steady, and this lovely bike. Northeast Ohio's gently rolling back roads are conducive to cycling for two. With plenty of open space and fair views, it's a lovely way to explore the state. A sure sign of springtime is the hum of a Harley out on the road for the first time in months, the passenger's arms wrapped around the driver's waist.

Step by Step

1 P.M.: Visit Harley Mecca, Southeast Harley-Davidson. Even if you don't own a motorcycle, you should make the trip to this unusual show-room/museum—you may end up leaving with one. Jeff Meyers's family has been operating Southeast Harley for 50 years, and in those 50 years the family has built up a showroom that is large—it's one of the biggest in the country—and filled with unexpected pleasures. Even advertising executives could see the uniqueness of Southeast Harley—they chose to feature the store in a 1992 Visa commercial.

Upon entering the showroom, you'll notice a display: Elvis Pres-ley's 1975 Harley-Davidson FIH, along with a vintage jumpsuit worn in concert by the King himself. If you're a fan of Elvis, you may hear angels singing when you first set eyes on what could only be called a shrine. For a die-hard Elvis fan, here is the Holy Grail of rock 'n' roll.

The showroom boasts an eclectic array of items: Buddy Holly's stage suit, a signed copy of the script for the feature film *Rain Man*, a guitar signed by the Birds, and another signed by the Eagles—pro-cured in honor of local musician and motorcycle enthusiast Joe Walsh, no doubt. Yet another surprising item is the dress worn by Judy Garland in *The Wizard of Oz*.

The main attraction is, of course, the extensive selection of mo-torcycles. Meander through the showroom and imagine riding the smallest to the largest of these machines, crafted in Milwaukee. This is the part of the day when you can put yourself in the saddle, see what it feels like atop a Harley, and let your dreams begin.

2 P.M.: You may think you're still dreaming when you see an old dining car from a train that seems misplaced in machine shop area of South-east. It's not a dream, and the burgers inside are heavenly. The Harley Cafe is fashioned from a circa 1946 Pullman dining car. From this tiny kitchen come big, juicy burgers. It was Elvis who brought you here, but the French fries, onion rings, coleslaw, and other standard diner food in this most unlikely restaurant will keep you coming back all on their own.

3 P.M.: After lunch, take a test drive. The staff at Southeast Harley can take you out on the road in style on a new Harley. While on the bike, you'll have time to think about how you can finance this bike and how you'll talk your partner into it. Hold on tight as the salesman tests speed, brakes, and maneuverability.

On your way out, make sure to browse through the Crow's Nest, the portion of the showroom devoted to Harley-Davidson clothes. The selection of leather jackets here is not limited just to biker leathers. Tailored and fitted high-quality jackets are surrounded by T-shirts, sweaters, ball caps, and every kind of cycling gear a body might need. And if you're a cyclist, your body does need some help. Helmets, leg guards, and safety equipment can be found here, too.

Variations:

FOR BIKERS ONLY: Once you leave Southeast Harley, hop on your hog and point your two wheels to SR43 South. This road takes you through country and industrial terrain past Reminderville, Aurora, and Streetsboro, and into Kent. Just past East Main Street on Franklin, you'll find Ray's Place, a rustic old watering hole where you'll feel right at home provided you get there early in the afternoon before the college kids start coming in. If you have an extra buck stick it in the jukebox, play some Dwight Yoakam, and enjoy the frosty beverage of your choice. Prices are low in this college town bar, and most of the time you can still pick up a beer for as little as a buck and a half.

Continue your journey west on Franklin till you hit SR91. This route provides more lovely scenery, taking you first through Hudson and then back up through Twinsburg, Solon, and Macedonia, where you can hop on SR82 to get back to where you started.

Directory

Ray's Place
135 Franklin St., Kent
330-673-2233

HOURS/AVAILABILITY:
Mon–Sat 11 a.m.–10 p.m.
(bar until 2:30 a.m.),
Sun 1 p.m.–10 p.m.
(bar until 2:30 a.m.)

Southeast Harley-Davidson
23105 Aurora Rd., Bedford
440-439-5300

HOURS/AVAILABILITY:
Mon–Thu 9 a.m.–6 p.m.,
Fri 9 a.m.–8 p.m.,
Sat 9 a.m.–5 p.m., Sun closed

Outing 37

LOVE GOLF

Season: Spring, Summer, Fall
Time: 6 hours ~ **Location:** South
Intimacy level: 1–2 ~ **Cost:** $–$$
Advance planning: Some

What You'll Do

❧ Play a round of Love Golf

❧ Have dinner and more love.

The closest I ever came to playing golf was the summer in college that I dated a guy named Omar, whose favorite pastime was, oddly, taking me for walks through deserted golf courses after dark and stealing a smooch somewhere around the ninth hole. I never understood this ritual, but in the summer of 1988—a drought season when the grass was so dry it would catch fire by the roadside—the green grass of the golf courses we visited in the evenings was a welcome escape from the hot summer days.

I don't feel guilty about my lack of passion for this game, however. At least not as long as John Tidyman and Lisa Metro walk the green. Tidyman, Cleveland's premier golf writer, has enough passion for the game to make up for 10 nongolfers. He is the only person I know who can discuss golf without losing my attention entirely. And when he's talking with Metro, his longtime golfing companion, about golf, you can almost hear the birds of love that chirp about their heads, and the sweet songs of devotion that spill out from each to the other. It's truly a beautiful thing to see these two in action. Each is a lover of golf, each is a strong, competitive personality, and yet they play together beautifully. How? Love Golf.

Step by Step

6 P.M.: The Tidyman/Metro game of Love Golf contains two crucial elements: nine holes, no scoring. Simply choose your favorite course—in this case, Skyland Golf Course in Hinckley—and schedule a nine-hole game. "Skyland is a wonderfully old course, constructed in 1922," says Tidyman. "It was built on rolling Medina county farmland, and the fairways are nice and wide." Tidyman thinks the staff there is the friendliest at any course he knows, making it the perfect atmosphere for a game between friends—or lovers. Tidyman and Metro play on weekend evenings when the golf course is "practically deserted" so that they can take their time.

Go into the game together with the expectation of playing a relaxing round of golf. "It's a nice way to spend a good couple of hours together," says Metro. "When you're with someone for a long time, you need a 'given' every week. This game gives us time to hang out together, and golf courses are relaxing places—they're green, and have all that oxygen."

"This game gives us time to hang out together, and golf courses are relaxing places— they're green, and have all that oxygen."

Leave the scoring behind to rule out any competitive edge that could otherwise ruin a relaxing evening such as this, and agree to simply indulge in the game—together. To illustrate just how noncompetitive their game is, Tidyman tells the story of one of their earlier games. "Lisa plays golf with a bunch of her girlfriends who apparently play by their own rules. I found this out when one day she and I were out playing love golf, and she hit one in the sand. Instead of getting a sand wedge out, she picked up the ball, dropped it on the green, and said, 'we don't do sand.'"

9 P.M.: When they're finished playing, the Tidyman/Metro twosome stops at KC's Four Corners Cafe for a casual dinner, settling into a booth amidst plenty of brass and ferns for a burger or a plate of veal Romano. You'll feel comfortable in golf pants or jeans here as families and neighborhood regulars eat and talk around you. After dinner, stop in the game room, where an electronic golf machine is connected with the Internet. Using a keyboard and a trackball, you can practice your swing against competitors all over the world with this machine.

In many ways, love golf is the glue that holds Tidyman's and Metro's relationship together. Look for them on a golf course some weekend evening: they're the couple laughing, joking, and dusting the sand off the ball as they drop it on the green. And one last piece of advice from Tidyman, "Never try to tell a broad about her swing."

Variations:

PUTTING ALONG: Not far from Skyland there's a different kind of golfer's haven: the putt-putt green at Goodtimes. Lovers can play just as challenging a game of golf here, where regular golf course obstructions like trees and sand are replaced by obstacles such as windmills and waterways (some are more than two inches deep). The putt-putt habit is much less expensive than its grown-up counterpart, and you can apply Tidyman's Love Golf philosophy to this game with ease. Goodtimes has additional diversions for adult patrons, including bumper boats and batting cages.

Directory

KC's Four Corners Cafe
7764 W. 130th St.,
Middleburg Hts.
440-845-1171
HOURS/AVAILABILITY:
Tue–Thu 11 a.m.–midnight,
Fri 11 a.m.–1 a.m.,
Sat noon–1 a.m.,
Sun–Mon 4 p.m.–10 p.m.

Goodtimes
33777 Chester Rd., Avon
440-937-6200
HOURS/AVAILABILITY:
Mon–Thu 6 p.m.–10 p.m.,
Fri 6 p.m.–midnight;
Sat–Sun noon–midnight;
times vary seasonally

Skyland Golf Course
2085 Center Rd. (SR 303),
Hinckley
330-225-5698
HOURS/AVAILABILITY:
April–mid-Nov dawn–dusk

Outing 38

TAKING A TOBOGGAN RIDE

Season: Winter ~ **Time:** 4–6 hours
Location: South ~ **Cost:** $–$$
Intimacy level: 1
Advance planning: None

What You'll Do

- Careen down a chute of ice ($10–$30).
- Warm up by a crackling fire with a mug of hot chocolate ($5–$10).

*M*y father used to tell stories about spending day after wintry day climbing up and sledding down the hill at Edgewater Park on a sled he maintained with tools from his father's workbench. Winters were colder then and more snow-filled, and as a nine-year-old kid in the depths of the Depression, he would spend an entire day careening down that wonderful hill. Modern technology can now guarantee a snowy toboggan ride, provided there's enough chill in the air, and the better part of an afternoon or evening can be spent whooshing down the slopes at the Mill Stream Run Chalet with the one you love.

Step by Step

3 P.M.: Plan to spend a thrilling afternoon at the chalet's toboggan chutes. Dress warmly in layers and make sure you have thick mittens or gloves, a hat, and a lot of energy. There's no need to bring a tobog-

gan; they are provided by the chalet. Ascend the stairway to the chutes, fly down on a toboggan, and repeat the process until you can't possibly climb anymore. "Invigorating" just begins to describe the thrill you'll experience atop a few pieces of wood as you clutch them for dear life while snow pelts you from above and ice sends you skidding underneath. These refrigerated half-pipes of ice operate during the cold months, serving up a thrilling ride and an athletic afternoon for you and your loved one.

Originally constructed in 1967, the twin ice chutes were the first of their kind in the world, guaranteeing Clevelanders a full season of ice, snow, and tobogganing. The chutes have since been updated and improved upon from an engineering standpoint, and the thrill is even more exciting as you experience a vertical drop of about 70 feet.

4:30 P.M.: Tired from the ride, walk over to the chalet for some snacks. The main feature of the chalet is its massive stone fireplace, where tobogganers warm their chilly hands and feet. Popcorn, hot dogs, and sundry other junk food is available, as well as hot chocolate and coffee. Warm up by the fire and see if you have the energy for one more run.

Variations:

SLEDDING—THE OLD-FASHIONED WAY: Spontaneity is an important part of sledding. Waking up to freshly fallen snow can give some people the urge to be the first to make tracks on the hill with a good old-fashioned sled. A good hill is not far away from you on Ohio's rolling landscape. Mike Barnhardt of the Metroparks suggests the following as perfect hills for avid sledders. (However, snow is not guaranteed):

"Invigorating" just begins to describe the thrill you'll experience atop a few pieces of wood as you clutch them for dear life while snow pelts you from above and ice sends you skidding underneath.

HUNTINGTON RESERVATION. The infamous lake-effect snow provides much of the necessary white stuff at the Huntington Hill just south of Lake Road and east of Porter Creek Road.

HINCKLEY RESERVATION. This park has plenty of lighting available for nocturnal sledders. Avid outdoors people can also try their hand at ice fishing and skating in the winter months.

NORTH CHAGRIN RESERVATION. Here sledders enjoy the ride at the Old River Farm area and the hills at Strawberry Pond. Both are lighted at night as well.

Directory

Chalet at Mill Stream Run Reservation

16200 Valley Parkway, Brecksville

440-572-9990

HOURS/AVAILABILITY:
Nov–Feb Thu and Fri 6 p.m.–10 p.m., Sat. noon–10:30 p.m., Sun noon–9 p.m.

Hinckley Reservation

Off Bellus and State Rds., Hinckley

216-351-6300

HOURS/AVAILABILITY:
Daily 6 a.m.–11 p.m.

Huntington Beach Reservation

Porter Creek Dr., Bay Village

216-351-6300

HOURS/AVAILABILITY:
Daily 6 a.m.–11 p.m.

North Chagrin Reservation

Buttermilk Falls Pkwy., Mayfield Village

216-351-6300

HOURS/AVAILABILITY:
Daily 6 a.m.–11 p.m.

Outing 39
BIKING

Season: Spring, Summer, Fall
Time: Overnight ~ **Location:** South
Intimacy level: 3 ~ **Cost:** $$–$$$$
Advance planning: Some–A lot

What You'll Do

- Bike on the Towpath Trail.
- Lunch with a lizard ($25–$30).
- Check into a rustic inn ($140–$160).

*M*iles of bike trails meander through the Cleveland area, and cycle enthusiasts are never at a loss for flat roads, rolling pathways, or rough terrain over which to pedal and sweat. Lovers young and old can take these trails at their own pace, finding hidden treasures along the way and establishing favorite routes to take for years to come. Here's one itinerary that includes sightseeing, lunch, and a night's stay at a bed-and-breakfast for cycling enthusiasts who like to take a journey.

The Ohio and Erie Canal Towpath Trail offers routes for every kind of cyclist, from the novice to the advanced. On this historic trail, you can travel from Cleveland to Akron and back again along the banks of the manmade Ohio and Erie Canal. The canal—once the hub of commerce in the Western Reserve—has been transformed into Ohio's first National Historic Area. Mill houses and lock-keepers' lodges along the way have been turned into museums, guesthouses, and visitors' centers. The towpath, once a rugged road traveled by mules pulling barges on the canal, is now a smooth asphalt pathway designed with bikers in mind.

Step by Step

11 A.M. Begin your bike trip at the Canal Visitor's Center. There is plenty of parking outside, with detailed trail maps and helpful park rangers inside. As an homage to the historic canal, the visitor's center houses a small museum devoted to the waterway and puts on canal lock demonstrations outside on weekends. The canal itself is a smooth, manmade waterway that is alive with river critters; its banks teem with wildflowers and weeds.

Bikers along the Towpath Trail have plenty of choices. For a day trip, take the trail south into Peninsula. Along the way, you'll be able to see Tinker's Creek Aqueduct and Alexander's Mill—a fully operational mill that is pretty to look at and interesting to tour. The Simon Frazee House, yet another historic stop along the way, demonstrates accurately what canal life was like 100 years ago.

Lovers young and old can take these trails at their own pace, finding hidden treasures along the way and establishing favorite routes to take for years to come.

Continue down the Towpath past SR82 to SR303 into Peninsula, which is literally a one-stoplight town, filled with charming shops, Victorian homes, and the Old Peninsula Inn Night Club. Now known as the Winking Lizard, this is a great place to refuel, sit back on the patio, and enjoy a burger, some ribs, or even a light salad. The Lizard is casual, so don't worry about feeling out of place in your biking shorts. Sitting under the sun, refreshed with food and drink, you can plot out the remainder of your biking day.

4:00 P.M. Backtrack on the Towpath Trail to the Inn at Brandywine Falls. Katie and George Hoy transformed this century home into a bed-and-breakfast 10 years ago to create a space that "gives the feeling that you're in the middle of the 1800s," according to Katie Hoy. There are six rooms to choose from, two of which have very 20th-century Jacuzzis, and the Inn has plenty of common areas indoors and out where guests can mingle and chat.

But the most spectacular feature here is Brandywine Falls, the fourth-tallest waterfall in Ohio. From the Inn, you can hear the falls gently roar, and a short walk across the way brings you face to face with the falls. You could spend hours holding hands and gazing at the falls and the surrounding scenery.

The Hoys keep a list of 19 nearby restaurants that you can walk or bike to, but on this kind of trip, a carryout dinner by the falls might be in order. Bring along a deck of playing cards or simply enjoy a quiet country evening outside, then let the falls lull you to sleep. Breakfast is served the next day, so load up on carbs for the return journey.

Variations:

If biking is your passion, pick up a copy of *25 Bicycle Tours in Ohio's Western Reserve* by Sally Walters. This guide is a must for cyclists interested in exploring new roads, Ohio history, and the area's natural beauty. Walters's guidebook is filled with detailed maps and directions pointing out areas of local interest along the way, and she's the book's photographer as well.

With this guidebook, you could schedule a summer exploring the Lake Erie islands and Northern Ohio and still have some uncovered trails to look forward to the following spring.

Directory

Cuyahoga Valley National Recreation Area/Canal Road Visitor's Center
Canal Rd. at Hillside Rd., Valley View
216-524-1497
HOURS/AVAILABILITY:
Canal Building:
Mon–Sun 8 a.m.–5 p.m.;
Happy Days Visitor Center
(South Bldg., Rt. 303):
Wed–Sun 8 a.m.–5 p.m.

Inn at Brandywine Falls
8230 Brandywine Rd., Sagamore Hills
330-467-1812
HOURS/AVAILABILITY:
Call ahead for booking.

Winking Lizard
1615 Main St., Peninsula
330-657-2770
HOURS/AVAILABILITY:
Mon–Thu 11 a.m.–10 p.m.,
Fri–Sat 11 a.m.–midnight,
Sun 11 am.–8 p.m.

Outing 40
CLIMB EVERY MOUNTAIN

 **Season:** Any ~ **Time:** 4–6 hours
Location: East
Intimacy: level: 1 ~ **Cost:** $–$$
Advance planning: Some

What You'll Do

⚑ Take a beginners' class to learn the basics of rock climbing ($15–$35).

⚑ Discuss your climb over a hearty Tap House meal.

NOTE: *Though anyone can enjoy rock climbing at the Cleveland Rock Gym, this outing assumes you'll want to take an introductory class. Call ahead to make reservations ($15 per person), and attend the class with shoes and gear appropriate to rock climbing— strong tennis or climbing shoes (which you can rent on-site), and a comfortable sweat suit that will protect you from scrapes if you fall. Since the gym can get breezy and cold at times, dress in layers.*

I took a trip to Ireland that changed my life. There, the people go "hill-walking" for a weekend. This entails nothing more than finding inexpensive lodging and walking the craggy, rocky landscape of Ireland, taking in the beautiful sights and undisturbed nature of that magical island. Since my return, I've been exploring our own landscape more and more, and talking with couples who spend plenty of weekends every year wandering through the hills, valleys, and mountains of this region.

I like these "nature couples" as I call them. Comfortable with each other, they're content to sleep in tents and explore nature, spending time alone without televisions or cell phones. Instead, they sit around a campfire by night, preparing for a day ahead filled with exploring. What a great way to be in love.

During the winter months—or on summer weekends when they just can't get away—these friends will travel to the Cleveland Rock Gym to take classes, learn new techniques, or just challenge themselves for a few hours. The Cleveland Rock Gym is an old warehouse designed with rock climbers in mind. Vertical trails with small rocks and challenging boulders entice the earthbound, while sheer cliffs beckon the more adventurous climbers who don't mind a long drop with only a nylon rope or two supporting them.

Step by Step

6:00 P.M.: Arrive at the Cleveland Rock Gym early enough to let them know you're there and pay your fees. A beginner's class costs about $15 per person, and you may want to rent some extra equipment while you're there (rental shouldn't cost more than $10–$20 total), including climbing shoes, gloves, or a helmet for the accident prone.

6:30 P.M.: Join your beginner's class. During this class, you'll learn the basics of rock climbing as an instructor gives you tips on safety, and shows you the ropes—literally—of rock climbing. On this journey in the gym, you'll ascend to 40 feet, meeting challenges along the way that are typical of a beginner's trail in the great outdoors. In a small group, you'll learn and climb for an hour, getting to know other climbers and practicing your technique.

If after your first class you're enthusiastic about rock climbing, sign up for classes on knot tying, using ropes, and managing falls. You can return to the gym again and again as the two of you gain experience. And perhaps you'll enjoy competing in some of the gym-sponsored events. Advanced climbers go off-site to learn about rappelling. The gym also sponsors—and provides information about—group hikes through trails in Northeast Ohio and beyond that are perfect for adventurous couples.

Climbing can quickly become a lifestyle for lovers of the outdoors. It's a relatively inexpensive and highly entertaining sport that is perfect for two people alone, or for a pair of lovers interested in getting out and meeting new people. And with the Cleveland Rock Gym just a short hike away you'll never be far from a climb.

8:00 P.M.: When the climb has worn you out, grab a bite at the nearby Tap House Bar and Grille. It's a favorite hangout of the rock-climbing staff, who will be happy to give you directions. The Tap House has a full menu of burgers, sandwiches, and heavy pastas to replenish your nutrients, as well as a hefty beer menu to wash it down with. It's part restaurant, part bar: you can usually find a local band playing rock and roll or blues on the weekends in this cozy neighborhood joint, and you might see a few of your fellow climbers ambling in for a post-workout snack.

Variations:

SOCIAL CLIMBING: Experience state-of-the-art climbing and electronically inspired weather in the great indoors at Newman Outfitters. This store, owned by relatives of actor Clevelander Paul Newman, has been a Newman family tradition for more than 100 years. The store's Solon location offers not only the gear you need for climbing in inclement weather; it offers the weather as well. An indoor storm chamber proves to customers the effectiveness of waterproof clothing by simulating an outdoor rainstorm. You can try out a kayak in the 3-foot kayaking pool inside the store, or try your skills on the rock-climbing wall. Spend an afternoon in this unusual retail store, and you'll feel like you've been away for a week.

Directory

Cleveland Rock Gym	Newman Outfitters	Tap House Bar and Grille
21200 St. Clair Ave., Bldg. B-3, Euclid	6025 Kruse Dr., Solon	937 E. 222nd St., Cleveland
216-692-3300	440-248-7000	216-261-3633
HOURS/AVAILABILITY: Mon–Fri 4 p.m.–10 p.m., Sat and Sun noon–6 p.m.	HOURS/AVAILABILITY: Mon–Thu 10 a.m.–9 p.m., Fri 10 am.–5 p.m., Sat 10 a.m.–7 p.m., Sun noon–5 p.m.	HOURS/AVAILABILITY: Mon–Sat 10:30 a.m.–2:30 a.m.

Outing 41
BUILDING CASTLES IN THE SAND

Season: Summer ~ **Time:** 4 hours
Location: West
Intimacy level: 1 ~ **Cost:** $
Advance planning: None or some

What You'll Do

🌢 Stock your picnic basket for a day at the beach ($10–$30).

🌢 Build a dream home made of sand.

🌢 Have your picnic lunch in the park.

Small children are satisfied with simple things. A few overturned buckets of moderately moist sand can be, for them, a delightful fairy castle. But adults in our society are not content with the tools—or the toils—of children. Instead, they arrive at the beach armed with grand ideas, intricate plans, and instruments for building. I once judged a sand castle tournament, expecting to find a series of predictably medieval-style structures. Instead, I was confronted with creations of every kind—a replica of Jacobs Field surrounded by an evil-looking serpent with the head of Art Modell, a woman made of sand who seemed to be rising from the beach, and a shipwreck so accurate I was tempted to reach in to look for hidden treasure. Taking the time to conceive of, plan for, and build a structure as fleeting as a sand castle can remind you of impermanence—of the importance of enjoying every moment to its fullest.

Step by Step

BEFORE YOU GO: Make a plan for your sand castle. Plan to build something the two of you fantasize about like a dream home, or car, or something you both admire, like a sand-relief of Michael Jordan sailing in a slam dunk. Pack a laundry basket with the tools you need, which might include:

> 2 buckets (one large and one small)
> a garden spade
> heavy-duty paint brushes—large and small
> a spray bottle
> throw-away camera

Depending on your design, you might want to incorporate additional household items—get creative. Cookie cutters, Jell-O molds, strainers, hubcaps, dust brooms. These all have applications in the fine art of sand castle building.

10 A.M.: Stock up a cooler with a picnic lunch from Lake Road Market. Because of this market's proximity to the Cleveland Yacht Club and a number of beach areas, there is a heightened awareness of the needs of the picnicker. Plenty of fresh deli salads, sandwich meats, hot dogs, and grilling supplies are kept in stock throughout the summer to accommodate the many beach bums who stroll through.

Cookie cutters, Jell-O molds, strainers, hubcaps, dust brooms. These all have applications in the fine art of sand castle building.

10:30 A.M.: Arriving at Huntington Beach early is essential. Fewer people will be there this early in the day, making it easier to stake out a space, and the sand will still retain some of its morning dew, an essential ingredient to work with. Choose a spot that is near the water, but not so close that you'll risk a flood. This way, you can add water as the day progresses without having to travel too far to get it.

Now, begin digging the foundation and building the castle. Teamwork is the key here, as you build the foundation and the supporting walls or curves and then add the finishing touches. Meet every failure as a new challenge.

You're likely to attract some attention from other folks on the beach, but don't be distracted. Stay focused. As the sun gets hotter, use the spray bottle to keep your creation moist. If you get tired of the project, walk around the beach to collect pebbles or driftwood to adorn your castle.

When you've finished, have someone on the beach take a picture of the two of you in front of your piece of beachfront real estate, and be sure to get plenty of close-ups of the structure itself. This is a showpiece, and if you apply enough photographic skill—and you've done an accurate enough job—you could even try to pass this off as your "summer home."

NOON: Once you've finished, take turns swimming in the lake (there will be children on the beach champing at the bit to jump on your castle the moment you leave). Find a spot from which to admire your castle and feast on a picnic lunch. While you eat, invent a fictitious family who lives in your castle and make up stories about what their life is like. Give them names, occupations, friends, and enemies. Then vow to build them another, bigger castle the next time you come.

Variations:

SNOW CASTLES: I've never understood the appeal of snowmen—three-tiered, overweight, and poorly dressed, with carrots for noses, to boot. I always prefer creating an icehouse—like Superman's Fortress of Solitude at the North Pole. The nice thing about snow castles is that they last much longer than their summer counterparts, and if you build one in your backyard and stock it with birdseed it will soon become a real house visited by neighborhood birds and squirrels. All the same instructions apply—sans the bikini—when building a snow castle. You just need to wait for that crunchy, moist snow to fall, fill a Thermos with hot chocolate, and get to work.

Directory

Huntington Beach Reservation
Porter Creek Dr., Bay Village
216-351-6300
HOURS/AVAILABILITY:
Daily 6 a.m.–11 p.m.

Lake Road Market
20267 Lake Rd., Rocky River
440-331-9326
HOURS/AVAILABILITY:
Mon–Fri 9 a.m.–7 p.m.,
Sat 9 a.m.–6 p.m.,
Sun noon–6 p.m.

Outing 42
MOVIE HOUSE MARATHON

Season: Any ~ **Time:** 1 weekend
Location: Downtown, East
Intimacy level: 1 ~ **Cost:** $$$–$$$$
Advance planning: Some

What You'll Do

- **FRIDAY EVENING:** Eat dinner and then see a film at the Cleveland Museum of Art; catch the late show at the Cedar Lee.

- **SATURDAY AFTERNOON:** Tower City Cinemas for a flick and some fast food.

- **SATURDAY EVENING:** An art film at the Cinematheque.

- **SUNDAY AFTERNOON:** A final critiquing session at Nighttown.

   NOTE: *Timing is everything on this outing, as you'll need to plan enough time to see a marathon of movies while still eating every once in a while. Use the following as a scheduling guide and spend an hour or so before you go planning your weekend.*

Dinnerannamovie? We've somehow managed to boil this statement down to a mundane mumble when there's nothing better to do, but never underestimate the possibilities of this evening—or, rather, weekend—out. Movies are powerful experiences that draw you in, eliciting strong emotions and forcing you into a discussion with your partner over coffee or dinner. Some films force us to confront personal issues or lead to an exchange of opinions that can help you to better know partner's moral makeup. On the other hand, movies can also be just a nice way to spend time together.

Theaters are scattered throughout the city, and in many cases one needn't travel more than 15 minutes to get to the nearest new release. Movies can be a last-minute quick fix for the question, "what do you want to do tonight?" But true movie buffs plan ahead, keeping their eyes on the paper for foreign flicks, art films, or festivals that take place outside the mainstream throughout the year. True film buffs can have fun by plotting an entire weekend full of film, film, film, trying out various theaters and films for a true marathon of their own making.

Step by Step

FRIDAY EVENING: Begin your weekend on Friday at the Cleveland Museum of Art. The museum shows films around 7 p.m. Generally, there is a single theme for the summer series, and throughout the year touring film series intermingle with the museum's own chosen themes for retrospectives. During the summer months, the museum keeps its doors open late on Wednesdays and Fridays, hosting courtyard guests who munch on fresh barbecue and listen to live music—a different band every week ranging from jazz to swing to folk and classical. In the cooler months, you can dine in at the museum café. A perfect evening at the museum includes a light dinner followed by a film in the theater.

After the museum film is over, plan to take in the late show at the Cedar Lee. The theater has a bohemian feel and offers unusual concession-stand foods that include freshly baked brownies and pastries to accompany the standard movie house fare of Twizzlers and Mike & Ike's. The Cedar Lee even has a liquor license if you desire a glass of wine during the film, turning a subtitled French import into an upscale version of the seventies' Smell-O-Rama.

Just next door, you'll find Parnell's Pub, a great after-movie stop for a pint of Guinness. Owned by two Irishmen—Declan Synnott and Sean Gromley—the place is small and pubbish and full of Irish hospitality.

SATURDAY AFTERNOON: Sleep in on Saturday because your movie house tour begins Saturday afternoon with a matinee at Tower City 11. The 11 theaters here boast a state-of-the-art sound system and plenty of choices. Grab a snack in the food court—pizza at Sbarro is always a good choice—and hop in the car to make the early show at the Cleveland Cinematheque.

SATURDAY EVENING: Since 1986, the Cinematheque has shown more than 250 films a year to an eclectic crowd of Clevelanders. "We always have a series going on," says John Ewing, the Cinematheque's director. "We have a healthy mix of new films, Cleveland premieres, classics, and second-run series." Throughout the year, visiting directors give lectures and new films are screened, and in the springtime cartoon buffs get a fix with *Animania*, a celebration of animated films and shorts. All proceeds from the screenings benefit the Cleveland Institute of Art, which operates the Cinematheque out of the Russell B. Aitken Auditorium.

SUNDAY EVENING: At Nighttown you can enjoy an after-film-marathon meal, or simply a cozy toddy in the pub. An Irish establishment, Nighttown is never short on conversationalists, so don't be surprised if your neighbor jumps in with an opinion or two.

In a series of rooms, each with its own personality, Nighttown serves up thick steaks, grilled salmon, and a nice array of appetizers and sandwiches. Most nights music by local musicians playing in the pub fills the air as well. A rich mixture of folk, traditional Irish music, and just plain old rock ballads adds to the buzz of this place. Bar patrons sip on cocktails in a moodily lit pub. It's a favorite first date spot and a regular stop for couples of every age.

Finish up the marathon weekend of films with a long walk outdoors through your own neighborhood. So much time indoors might have you feeling a bit sluggish. Take some time to talk over the films you've seen and the theaters you've been in. Then plot your next attack on Cleveland's film houses.

Variations

BIG NIGHT: If you missed Stanley Tucci's film *Big Night*, make sure you rent it. In this hilarious film, two brothers try to save their restaurant by spending the very last of their money on a lavish, multi-course traditional Italian meal whose centerpiece is a pasta extravaganza called il timpano. At the Palazzo two sisters—Gilda and Carla Carnecelli—re-create this lavish meal a few times a year and show the movie during dinner. Clevelander Sam Hutchins, who was the location scout for *Big Night*, is a fan of the Palazzo himself. Hutchins recounts that Mrs. Tucci (Stanley's mother) made three timpanos for the filming of *Big Night*, and that the crew was allowed to eat the leftover one—cold. "With all due respect to Mrs. Tucci, I would've preferred the Palazzo meal, myself," says Hutchins. Call the Palazzo for dates and times.

Direct Your Own

CREATE YOUR OWN FILM: The best part of romance isn't necessarily the fun you have while you're in the most romantic stage of your relationship; the best part is the lasting memories you'll create while you're there. These memories can act as kindling throughout the course of a long-term relationship, offering flashes of the potential of your love when the fires occasionally burn low.

Photo albums, journals, and now videotapes serve as great reminders to you—and as examples to your children—of the ideal of love you have created for yourselves. Take some time every few years to wrap these memories into a short, cohesive package. Digital cameras will make this effort easier for us in the future, but while they're perfecting the technology, you can upgrade your memories onto videotape, or even onto your hard drive if that's what you desire.

Upgrade your memories onto videotape, or even onto your hard drive if that's what you desire.

Friends of mine had documented their courtship and early marriage well with photographs, and the husband, Pete Kwiatkowski, wanted to convert these images into a video. Knowing his wife would be angry if he spent a great deal of money on the video, Pete swindled me into convincing his wife that I had produced the video for free. I feel the guilt every time his wife, Ellen, mentions the gift, but the lie is worth it when I remember how much it meant to her the Christmas she received it.

In addition to involving accomplices, Pete's video took a lot of planning. Collating photos or videotapes into such a package requires plenty of editing. You'll want to storyboard the pictures so that they follow a logical progression of some sort, and make sure they are timed well with the music you choose. Typically, you'll want to allow 3–5 seconds per photo, and you won't want your video to exceed 10 minutes. In reality, 5 minutes might be just enough, but have the tape dubbed onto a longer VHS cassette so you can add to it in the years to come.

This process takes up not only time but space as well—two things that make it difficult to hide from a close loved one if you're making this a surprise. Be inventive or devise some reason for being out of the house a night or two a week until you're done, perhaps staying late at the office—where you'll have to conceal your new-found sensitivity from your co-workers.

Once your storyboard is done and timed, take your photos,

music, and storyboard to a videographer who can transfer the photos to video for you. This process takes at least one week, so if you're trying to hit a certain deadline be sure to give them at least two weeks' notice.

Plan a quiet evening to view the tape or invite a few close friends and family over. Along with the videocassette, present a tape or CD with the music you used in the video. Make the evening seem casual, pop up some popcorn, and with all the nonchalance you can muster, pop in the tape. You'll likely conjure up some tears, but don't worry—these are the good kind of tears.

Directory

Cedar Lee Theatre
2163 Lee Rd.,
Cleveland Heights
440-717-4696
HOURS/AVAILABILITY:
Call for movie times.

Charles Stewart Parnell Pub
2167 Lee Rd.,
Cleveland Heights
216-321-3469
HOURS/AVAILABILITY:
Daily 4 p.m.–2 a.m.

Cleveland Cinematheque
11141 East Blvd., Cleveland
216-421-7450
HOURS/AVAILABILITY:
Call for movie times.

Cleveland Museum of Art
11150 East Blvd., Cleveland
216-421-7350
HOURS/AVAILABILITY: Summer patio: Wed and Fri 7 p.m.; Call for concert times and special events.

Nighttown
12383 Cedar Rd., Cleveland
Heights
216-795-0550
HOURS/AVAILABILITY:
Mon–Sat 11:30 a.m.– midnight, Sun 10 a.m.– midnight

Palazzo
10031 Detroit Rd., Cleveland
216-651-3900
HOURS/AVAILABILITY:
Thu–Sat 5 p.m.–10 p.m., catering for private events.

Tower City Cinemas
The Avenue at Tower City
230 W. Huron Rd., Cleveland
440-717-4697
HOURS/AVAILABILITY:
Call for movie times.

Outing 43

LEAP TALL BUILDINGS IN A SINGLE BOUND

Season: Any ~ **Time:** 6 hours
Location: Downtown and above Northeast Ohio
Intimacy level: 1 ~ **Cost:** $$$–$$$$
Advance planning: Some

What You'll Do

- Climb up a pyramid for a bird's-eye view of the lake ($36).
- Shoot straight to the heights of Metropolis at Tower City ($10).
- Lunch high atop a moored ship ($25–$35).
- Take a champagne flight above the city ($90).

NOTE: *Book a Saturday flight with Cleveland AirSports at least a week in advance.*

or their honeymoon, my parents drove through thick February snows to a cabin in the Smoky Mountains. They arrived late in the evening, and, well, it being their wedding night I don't suppose they took too much time to take in the surrounding view. The next morning, however, my mother discovered that their honeymooners' cabin was perched high atop the cliffs of a steep gorge. So much for the honeymoon—my mother is afraid of heights.

This outing isn't for the fainthearted or the acrophobic. But if you have no fear, then you've got friends in high places in Cleveland. Three spots in downtown Cleveland offer progressively higher points from which to view the city. Start at the bottom and work your way up as you see increasingly spectacular views in your daylong journey to the top.

Step by Step

11 A.M.: Searching for ever greater heights? Start at the Terminal Tower. When it was opened to the public in June of 1930, the Cleveland Union Terminals Project was said to be "the greatest specimen of peacetime engineering achieved since the Panama Canal." My grandfather worked on the project, contracting his company to help dig the massive base for this great civic project. When it was built, the Terminal Tower was the second-tallest building in the world, outdone only by New York's Woolworth Building. This record would hold for 40 years, until the completion of the Sears Tower in Chicago.

The building's impact on Cleveland culture is lasting. Superman was born under the shadow of the great tower, as Dennis Dooley, co-author of *Superman at Fifty* notes: "When [Jerry] Siegel and [Joe] Shuster were kids growing up in the Glenville area in the early 1930s, the Terminal Tower was the tallest building between New York and Chicago. So when they imagined Superman leaping tall buildings in a single bound, it was very likely that it was the Terminal Tower that came to mind. It defined their idea of a skyscraper."

In fact, one of the earliest Superman comic strips refers not to Metropolis, but Cleveland itself, says Dooley: "The lasting image of the Terminal Tower was emblazoned on their early memory." Even in today's comic strips and on the silver screen Metropolis architec-

"When they imagined Superman leaping tall buildings in a single bound, it was very likely that it was the Terminal Tower that came to mind. It defined their idea of a skyscraper."

ture carries the signature of the Art Deco movement that inspired some of the great buildings of downtown Cleveland.

The Terminal Tower extends 708 feet into thin air, a no-brainer for Superman, but we mere mortals must ride a series of elevators to ascend to the observation deck, open Saturdays and Sundays from 11 a.m. to 4 p.m. The trip is worth the effort. From this glass-walled circular perch you can see Greater Cleveland for almost 40 miles on a clear day. If you're not equipped with Superman's extraordinary vision, telescopes are on hand to help you locate your neighborhood or to gaze just across Public Square.

On your way out of the Terminal Tower, take a short detour through Memorial Plaza, which was refurbished when the Key Center was built, creating an even more beautiful home for the War

From this glass-walled circular perch you can see Greater Cleveland for almost 40 miles on a clear day.

Memorial. Its centerpiece is a sculpture by Marshall Fredericks called *Peace Arising from the Flames of War*. (It's also known as *The Fountain of Eternal Life*.) Originally commissioned in 1964 and restored in 1989 in conjunction with the creation of Key Plaza, this elegant sculpture radiates hope, depicting a feminine figure arising from flames, her arms outstretched to the sky. Take a long moment to reflect on this image meant to represent humanity (fallen soldiers) rising from the flames of war.

1 P.M.: If vertigo hasn't yet set in, plan to have lunch on the upper deck at Hornblower's Barge and Grill, another of Cleveland's more unique high places. From this crow's-nest perch, the view of the lake, Burke Lakefront Airport, and downtown is spectacular. The barge is moored tightly, but the gentle roll of the lake is still perceptible. Hornblower's menu features plenty of seafood and light lunch fare—you'll want to lunch lightly in preparation for your next stop—but even more enjoyable is a comfortable spot in the sunlight, listening to the waves lap against the side of this great old boat.

3 P.M.: Just across the way is Burke Lakefront Airport, where you've chartered a Champagne Flight. For a surprisingly low all-inclusive fee (usually around $90), Cleveland AirSports provides a basket of truffles and a split of champagne. They'll also take your photo before they place you in a four- or six-seater aircraft for a sightseeing flight around the Cleveland area.

"Flights are usually about 30 minutes, and you can choose where you'd like to go," says owner George Katsikas. A typical flight will take you out over the lake toward the Avon stacks, and off to the south of the city for a bit, and then cut up along the shores of Bratenahl while you sip on champagne and eat chocolates.

"Our small planes can stay at a low altitude, so you can really see a lot," says Katsikas. "I recommend the sunset tour, though," he adds. "You can depart just before dusk and watch the sun as it is extinguished right into the water."

Make sure to steal a kiss in the back of the plane while the pilot isn't looking. As the plane lands, think back on your dizzying day and take note: Has your love now reached new heights?

Directory

Cleveland AirSports
1501 Marginal Rd., Cleveland
216-241-2417
HOURS/AVAILABILITY:
Call for appointment

Hornblower's Barge and Grill
1151 North Marginal Rd., Cleveland
216-363-1151
HOURS/AVAILABILITY:
Mon–Thu 11 a.m.–10 p.m.,
Fri and Sat 11 a.m.–midnight

Terminal Tower Observation Deck
50 Public Square, Cleveland
216-771-0033
HOURS/AVAILABILITY: Saturdays 11 a.m.–4 p.m.

Outing 44
LET'S GO BOWLING!

Season: Any ~ **Time:** 2–4 hours
Location: South
Intimacy level: 1 ~ **Cost:** $–$$
Advance planning: None

What You'll Do

➤ Shop for bowling supplies and gear ($10–$50), then bowl, bowl, bowl ($5–$10).

NOTE: *You can make a reservation to bowl at Parma Recreation. Call ahead for times, as bowling league schedules fluctuate.*

*B*owling is like an old friend. It's always there for you, it's easy to get comfortable with it after a long absence, and once you have, you wonder why you don't keep in touch with it more often. The lure of this indoor sport is mesmerizing. It seems so simple, and yet it's challenging. The challenge is addicting. Trading turns with your partner, sharing a bag of chips and a soda, the hours can pass quickly. Atmosphere is the most crucial element of a successful bowling outing, however, and to truly achieve atmosphere, you need the proper equipment, and just the right alley.

Step by Step

3 P.M.: Begin the bowling experience at Vince's Pro Shop. Owner Vince Dailey stocks 65 different kinds of bowling balls alongside a wide se-

lection of bowling shirts and accessories. But most importantly, Vince stocks bowling shoes. I don't know about you, but my only real turn-off to bowling is that moment when you rent—and first put on—bowling alley shoes. Even if you plan to bowl only a few times a year, the shoes are worth the investment—a low-end pair costs under $30—for peace of mind alone, and they're actually kind of cool (great for wearing around the house, too).

4 P.M.: Bowl. The sign in front of Parma Recreation spells out the word BOWLING in large, rectangular letters. Owner Jodi Bailey says the sign has been spotted on *The Drew Carey Show*. Inside, each of the 12 lanes is fitted with an above-ground ball return and the original benches that were installed with the alley more than 60 years ago. At the bar area, you can pick up a long-neck beer and some snacks to munch on while you play. Scoring is manual at Parma Recreation— no fancy electronic scoring schemes here, which might explain why a game of bowling still costs a mere $1.50.

During the week, Parma Recreation is dedicated mostly to bowling leagues—from schoolchildren to serious adult bowlers. But when Friday and Saturday nights roll around, the place is hopping with couples and friends out to enjoy a few games. You can call ahead to make reservations or wait a few minutes at the bar for a lane to open up. It's worth the wait. The sound of balls rolling across the highly polished wooden lane, then smashing against a set of pins will mesmerize as you watch the ballet only bowlers know.

Directory

Parma Recreation Bowling Lanes
5721 Ridge Rd., Parma
440-884-0840
HOURS/AVAILABILITY:
Open bowling: Tue 4 p.m.–9 p.m.,
Wed–Fri, 2 p.m.–6 p.m. and
10 p.m.–midnight, Sat 3 p.m.–
6 p.m. and 10 p.m.–midnight,
Sun noon–9 p.m.

Vince's Pro Shop
5857 Ridge Rd., Cleveland
440/886-4142
HOURS/AVAILABILITY:
Mon–Wed noon–9 p.m.,
Thu and Fri noon–5 p.m.,
Sat noon–6 p.m.

Outing 45
PROGRESSIVE DINNER

Season: Spring, Fall, Winter

Time: 7 hours ~ **Location:** Near West

Intimacy level: 1 ~ **Cost:** $$–$$$

Advance planning: Some

What You'll Do

- Appetizers at Johnny Mango ($10).
- Soup at Great Lakes Brewing Company ($10).
- Salads at Heck's ($20).
- Main course at the Flying Fig ($40–$50).
- After-dinner cheeses at the Wine Bar ($20–$25).

NOTE: *Plan your schedule carefully and make reservations for each stop. Explain what you're doing to make sure they understand that you're on a schedule and will need to be seated promptly.*

New lovers can never sit still. Their heightened state of excitement requires continual movement and gratification of the senses in excess. Sitting politely through seven courses is simply unbearable for these fidgets. Indulge in—or bring back—this state of high-flown passion with an indulgent walk through the eateries of Ohio City.

The idea for this progressive romantic dinner was provided by a guy who admitted to dining most frequently at a restaurant recognizable by its trademark: a big fake bell. Instinctively I knew that this was a man in possession of a hungry romantic soul. I rushed him immediately to

Johnny Mango in Ohio City in an attempt to introduce him to the variety of nourishment that surrounds him in this vibrantly ethnic community. The experiment failed, however, and I suspect this man continues to suppress his true desires by making a run to the border, where processed cheese foods are used with reckless abandon.

Elevate your dining experiences and enrich your relationships with added romance by making your way to Ohio City to enjoy five courses in one evening. Along the way, you'll take in all the charm of this old-world neighborhood and meet a host of chefs, proprietors, and "regulars" who make up this colorful community.

Step by Step

6 P.M.: Start out with appetizers at Johnny Mango, where the specialties are international foods and exotic blended juice drinks. To gain energy for your walk and whet your palate, order a Pelican Kiss, a refreshing drink made of cranberry, ginger, and apples. Quiz the waiter about specials of the day and order an eggplant spread or a dish of fried plantains, but don't pass on the fresh guacamole and chips—it's the best in town. Johnny Mango's bright colors and the clouds floating on the ceiling will put you in a lighthearted mood, and soon you'll be ready to conquer Ohio City.

7 P.M.: Take your conquering spirit to the Great Lakes Brewing Company for your second course. Filled with a hearty after-work crowd that generally includes a smattering of fresh-off-the-boat Irishmen who are there to verify that Great Lakes brew is the "real thing," Great Lakes is among the best pubs in Cleveland. A cup of hearty beer-cheese soup served with crusty dipping bread is a slightly heavy appetizer for one, but shared by two it will leave you wanting more. The mixture of sharp Stilton cheese mingled with a slightly bitter beer taste is a decadent way to introduce cholesterol into your system. Fear not, love burns calories, and so does walking.

8 P.M.: Heck's Cafe, around the corner and down a few blocks, will be your next stop for salad. It is set in a century-old brick building that stands proudly on Bridge Avenue. There always seems to be some hustle and bustle outside of Heck's, and inside diners enjoy an atmosphere of exposed brick, high windows, and painted window-panes. Much care has been taken to maintain the Victorian charm of the rooms that make up the restaurant. Fresh, light, seasonal, and whimsical, each salad has a personality of its own. Choose from an array of greens including the requisite Caesar, or portobello mush-

room and beef on Romaine. Two salads stand out on this menu. The Piraeus salad is a Grecian medley of chicken, feta cheese, and apricots mixed in a vinaigrette; the most exotic of the greenery is the Key West mango salad, featuring mixed field greens, mangos, and seasonal vegetables tossed in a raspberry vinaigrette.

9 P.M.: Entrees at the Flying Fig. Eating at the Flying Fig is a trendy, flavorful experience. The open room is usually abuzz with patrons, while the staff scurries in and out of the kitchen with Mediterranean dishes full of spice and flavor. Bartenders expertly pour drinks or glasses of wine from an inventive list.

10:30 P.M.: After-dinner sophistication. With its exposed brick, generous oak bar, and candlelit crevices, the Market Avenue Wine Bar offers the best of Sausalito, Italy, and France. Downstairs, the bar is usually crowded with a friendly gang of interested patrons who quiz the knowledgeable bartenders on the ins and outs of the many wines on the menu. Upstairs a Victorian parlor that resembles Aunt Bea's living room is a comfortable setting for an after-dinner chat. Order a plate of cheeses and ask the waiter to suggest a good port. In short order you'll be talking pleasantly, munching on cheese, and sipping on a well-chosen drink.

Directory

Flying Fig
2523 Market Ave., Cleveland
216-241-4243
HOURS/AVAILABILITY:
Tue–Sun 5 p.m.–1 a.m.,

Great Lakes Brewing Co.
2516 Market Ave., Cleveland
216-771-4404
HOURS/AVAILABILITY:
Mon–Thu 11:30 a.m.–10:30 p.m. (bar until midnight),
Fri and Sat 11:30 a.m.–11:30 p.m. (bar until 1 a.m.),
Sun 3 p.m.–9 p.m.

Heck's Cafe
2927 Bridge Ave., Cleveland
216-861-5464
HOURS/AVAILABILITY:
Mon–Wed 11:30 a.m.–10:30 p.m., Thu 11:30 a.m.–11:30 p.m., Fri–Sat 11:30 a.m.–midnight,
Sun 11 a.m.–9:30 p.m.

Johnny Mango
3120 Bridge Ave., Cleveland
216-575-1919
HOURS/AVAILABILITY:
Mon–Fri 11 a.m.–10 p.m.,

Sat 9 a.m.–11 p.m.,
Sun 9 a.m.–10 p.m.

Market Avenue Wine Bar
2526 Market Ave., Cleveland
216-696-9463
HOURS/AVAILABILITY:
sun, Tue and Wed 4 p.m.–midnight, Mon 6 p.m.–midnight, Thu and Fri 4 p.m.–1 a.m.,
Sat 2:30 p.m.–1 a.m.

Outing 46
BE JEWELED

Season: Any
Location: Downtown/East ~ **Time:** 1 day
Intimacy level: 3 ~ **Cost:** $$–$$$
Advance planning: Some–A lot

What You'll Do

- Hire a local designer to hand craft a piece of personalized jewelry.
- Present your love with a trinket ($1–$3).
- Visit a sparkling gem exhibit ($15).
- Window shop at an exclusive mall.
- Dine at the jewel in the crown of the East Side ($50–$100).

NOTE: *Planning a personalized piece of jewelry can take some time. Consult with a jeweler at least a month in advance to allow time for design and craftsmanship.*

*L*ove is like a rock. Like the 69.42-karat rock given to Elizabeth Taylor by her then-husband Richard Burton. At the time of the purchase, the "Cartier-Burton Diamond" was valued at $1,050,000. Materialistic or not, like it or not, jewelry is a concrete symbol of love and commitment.

However, you needn't go to the expense that Burton did to say "I love you." When money fails you, rely on resourcefulness. To the casual onlooker, jewelry is just adornment. But to the wearer, it is adored. Jewelry, because of its intimate contact with our skin, and its weight and feel is meaningful each time it is worn. So instead of just purchasing jewelry, make sure you create a symbol.

One surefire way to do this is by having jewelry made. It's not as complicated as it seems. A friend of mine, Tony, is from Australia. He collects opals every time he visits home. Apparently, opal hunting is a favorite pastime of Australians, as these iridescent gems are sprinkled throughout the countryside rather liberally. After dating a friend of mine for a few months, he noticed that she liked to wear crosses. He contacted a jewelry maker to fashion a cross that he had designed. Placed at its center was one of his prized opals. The result was a thoughtful, captivating gift.

Most jewelry stores have a designer on staff who can assist with custom-made jewelry, but there is also a thriving community of jewelry makers in town whose work ranges from the whimsical to the exquisite. Often freelance jewelry makers will take a real interest in what it is you're trying to accomplish, and will take great care in creating a special keepsake that's within your budget.

Step by Step

BEFORE YOU GO: Charles Rivchun & Sons Inc is a great place to start your search. Located in the Citizen's building, Rivchun is home to a treasure trove of jewelry and other adornments. Present them with your idea and your budget, and they'll help you design just the right ring, bracelet, or necklace.

There is a protocol that goes with presenting such a gift. You are not giving an ordinary gift—you're bestowing a memory. This calls for a ceremony. Keith and Cheri are a happily married couple. Keith pulled off quite a caper, however, in asking Cheri to marry him. Jewelry, of sorts, was involved. I'll let him tell the story . . .

Jewelry is meaningful each time it is worn.
So instead of just purchasing jewelry,
make sure you create a symbol.

I knew for quite some time that I was going to ask Cheri to marry me, and I was pretty sure it would be at Christmas in 1994. I wanted it to be a surprise, so I started to lay the foundation for my deception early.

First I was helped when Ameritech downsized its PR department, leaving me to look for full-time, permanent work. This little development really made Cheri believe any proposal would be delayed indefinitely.

I took another step, though. Once when we were watching TV, one of those God-awful De Beers diamond ads come on—the ones that use shadows of people wearing diamonds and extol the virtues of spending two months' salary on an engagement ring. Well, one commercial talked about a diamond bracelet to mark a couple's 10th anniversary. I have always scoffed at these ads, and this time I turned to Cheri and said, "To me, a good 10th anniversary gift is a Silverstone skillet. You give it to your wife and say, 'Fry me up an omelet.'" Now Cheri thinks I'm totally down on marriage, and the prospects of our union seem a bit more diminished.

Fast forward to Christmas. I scour Northeast Ohio for a Silverstone skillet. I check probably half a dozen places, finally finding one at the old U.S. Merchandise in Rocky River. It had to be Silverstone in keeping with my earlier comment. I also found an imitation gold key chain, took off the garish thingy hanging from it, and put a set of my house keys on the ring. The final piece was a small cartoon book—the kind that has simple animation to it as you flip through it. This one had a cat (I had two, she had two) popping out of a chimney and wishing a person "Merry Christmas."

In the animation book, I made the cat also ask: "Will you marry me?" I used red and green ink in keeping with the season. The book is wrapped separately, but is inside the package with the skillet. The gold key chain is a separate item that will be given last.

Christmas Eve comes, the two of us and her family gather at Cheri's apartment, open presents, then they leave so we can open our own private gifts to each other. I rush through her gifts to me. I'm obviously anxious and excited.

First, she opens the large package and sees the skillet. Her first words: "I hope there's humor in this." I urge her to open the small item (the book). She does, scans it several times and finally sees the proposal. That's when the tears start.

Finally, I give her the small present with the keys in it. After she opens it, I say, "Until we can get you a real engagement ring, I want you to have this gold ring with my house keys. My house is now our home."

She said yes, and the rest is history.

As a postscript, I had landed a full-time consulting job at a PR agency about this time. Within several weeks, a ring and wedding band were selected, and she got her "real" engagement ring in January 1995. We were married September 16, 1995, and she still keeps me around!

10 A.M., DAY OF OUTING: Though Keith took the idea to extremes, you can have a lot of fun incorporating a little inspired levity into the giving of a special gift. Make him or her hungry for it. Tease them. Start out the day by bestowing a mundane gift: a cheap pair of earrings, or a trinket necklace. The tackier the better—extra points if a birthday or anniversary is involved. Make like that's it; that's all your love is getting.

3 P.M.: Add insult to injury, choose that afternoon for a special trip to the Wade Gallery of Gems and Jewels at the Cleveland Museum of Natural History. Resentment should mount as you walk her through the more than 1,500 precious gems, jewels, gold carvings, and multicolored diamonds on display. The gallery is set in a cavelike environment designed to enhance the geological aspect of the gem walk, but in your case, it will cement in her mind the idea that you're nothing short of a caveman. You're doing well.

5 P.M.: Take a drive to Beachwood Place to window shop, encouraging her to try on some jewelry—make a game of it. Point out a Cartier necklace and say something really annoying like "Honey, this is almost just like that thing I gave you today."

7 P.M.: In a sting operation like this, it's important to know your limits, and to nudge them to the extreme. To take the edge off—and set the next part of your evening up—make reservations at Moxie. This particular restaurant is tactically important for a few reasons. First, it's a great place to eat. Fresh game, sauces to write home about (a wasabi that will make you cry), and a dessert menu that screams decadence will work to assuage the harm you've done today. But, more importantly, it's a well-lit, very public place. You'll need this advantage when, at last, you present your real gift, as it will not only help her to see the beauty of the gift you've given, but it will allow her to display it to the tables nearby. The true self-indulgent pleasure of jewelry lies not only in having it, but in showing it off. Once onlookers have smiled their approval, you'll be quickly elevated from caveman back to loved one.

Variations:

LOW-BUDGET JEWELRY: So you don't have a month's salary to spend on a necklace? No boat to trade in for a diamond-chip tie clip? Maybe it really is the thought that counts, so do your shopping at Big Fun where there's plenty of jewelry—plastic jewelry, jewelry that squirts water, candy jewelry, and whimsical lapel pins—to choose from. Make up a treasure chest of jewelry (don't miss the spider rings), chocolate coins, and other surprises. The points you lose on not getting real jewelry, you'll regain on creativity.

Directory

Beachwood Place
26300 Cedar Rd., Beachwood
216-464-9460
HOURS/AVAILABILITY:
Mon–Fri 10 a.m.–9 p.m.,
Sat 10 a.m.–7:30 p.m.,
Sun noon–6 p.m.

Big Fun
1827 Coventry Rd.,
Cleveland Hts.
216-371-4386
HOURS/AVAILABILITY:
Sun–Wed noon–6 p.m.,
Thu noon–8 p.m, Fri–Sat
11 a.m.–9 p.m. Sometimes
closed on Monday; hours vary
by season; please call ahead.

Charles Rivchun and Sons Jewelry
850 Euclid Ave., Suite 506,
Cleveland
216-781-0999
HOURS/AVAILABILITY:
Mon–Fri 9:30 a.m.–4:30 p.m.,
Sat 9 a.m.–2:30 p.m.

Moxie
3355 Richmond Rd., Beachwood
216-831-5599
HOURS/AVAILABILITY:
Mon–Thu 11:30 a.m.–2:30
p.m. and 5:30 p.m.–10 p.m.,
Fri 11:30 a.m.–2:30 p.m.
and 5:30 p.m.–11 p.m.,
Sat 5:30 p.m.–11 p.m.,

Sun 5 p.m.–9 p.m.

**Wade Gallery
of Gems and Jewels**
1 Wade Oval Drive, Cleveland
216-231-4600
HOURS/AVAILABILITY:
Mon–Sat 10 a.m.–5 p.m.,
Sun noon–5:00 p.m.

Outing 47
ALTRUISTS IN LOVE

Season: Any
Location: Downtown ~ **Time:** 3 hours
Intimacy level: 1 ~ **Cost:** $
Advance planning: Some–A lot

What You'll Do

🏹 Spend a morning helping with horses and disabled kids at Fieldstone Farm.

🏹 Have lunch at the Mustard Seed Market.

NOTE: *Be sure to call ahead to tour Fieldstone Farm. Also, make sure you wear sturdy boots and clothes you don't mind getting dirty.*

y parents—and all their friends—were always very involved in volunteer efforts. Some groups they belonged to separately, others they enjoyed working on together. These activities gave them something outside themselves to focus on and at the same time kept them aware of the important aspects of their relationship. Being involved in helping other couples and families facing hardship helped to keep any hardships my parents might have suffered in perspective. Feeding the homeless once a week surely helped my mother to appreciate every morsel of food she put on our family table. I'm certain that these activities also kept my parents' love and respect for each other strong.

Step by Step

BEFORE YOU GO: Once a year—or once a week—take some time out from being a couple that indulges each other to be a couple that helps others. Pick a Sunday evening and sit down together to plan your giving strategy for the year. Which charities do you both like? Is there a local organization that appeals to you? Mix some Machiavellianism in with your altruism and get your accountant on the phone to find out how your giving strategy might help you with the taxes this year. Spend an hour or two to focus completely on a strategy for helping others. You might find out some things about each other you never knew.

A WEEK BEFORE YOU GO: Call ahead to Fieldstone Farm to make reservations for a tour. Fieldstone Farm is an unusual horse farm where disabled children are the center of attention. Here, kids with disabilities of every kind—whether they're learning disabled, vision impaired, or severely handicapped—work with people and horses for therapy and fun. A not-for-profit organization, Fieldstone depends on professionals and novices alike to help with everything from grooming the horses (and, yes, cleaning their stalls), to working with the kids, to training the horses for this special work.

So, whether you're a horse trainer by trade, or just a couple who likes to be in the outdoors with these beasts of burden, you'll enjoy touring Fieldstone. "We provide riding lessons to kids with disabilities," explains the farm's executive director, Laura Barnett. "By working with horses, kids increase their self-esteem, gain independence, and even improve muscle coordination and posture."

On your tour, you'll see kids riding and encounter the volunteers

Here, kids with disabilities of every kind— whether they're learning disabled, vision impaired, or severely handicapped—work with people and horses for therapy and fun.

and staff who work with them. And, of course, you'll also get to see the horses. While you're there, decide if you'd like to become a regular volunteer at Fieldstone. Laura Barnett says she sees all kinds of people helping out on the farm. "We will train volunteers to work with the horses," she says. "I've seen people who have never ridden a horse before learn to lead a horse around the ring."

If you do decide to come back and become a regular volunteer, you'll take a three-hour training course which teaches safety, first aid, and working with horses. Perhaps you'll decide to make a regular commitment to volunteer together at Fieldstone once a month—or once a quarter. They'll be delighted to have the two of you back, and you'll have a wonderful experience to look forward to regularly.

NOON: Feed yourself—and your altruism—with a visit to the Mustard Seed Market and Cafe in nearby Solon. All products sold at the Mustard Seed meet strict standards for organic, chemical-free foods. The store also strives to work with local farmers and growers to ensure that the local community is involved and utilized. Chef Mark Shari creates daily specials in the sit-down café that take advantage of the freshest seasonal foods and the most unique spices available through the market to provide you with an exotic organic meal.

Directory

Fieldstone Farm
16497 Snyder Rd., Bainbridge
440-708-0013
HOURS/AVAILABILITY:
Mon–Sat 8:30 a.m.–5 p.m.

Mustard Seed Market and Cafe
6025 Kruse Dr., Solon
440-519-3600
HOURS/AVAILABILITY:
Mon–Fri 11 a.m.–2:30 p.m.
and 5 p.m.–10 p.m.,
Sat 10 a.m.–11 p.m.,
Sun 11 a.m.–5 p.m.

Outing 48
ALL ABOARD!

Season: Spring, Summer, Fall
Time: 8 hours ~ **Location:** South, Far South
Intimacy level: 1 ~ **Cost:** $$
Advance planning: None

What You'll Do

 ❧ Climb aboard a vintage train.

 ❧ Tour a local castle and its gardens.

On my wall is a survey in which I participated at the age of four. It was a fill-in-the-blank providing beginnings to such sentences as "My biggest problem is . . ." and listing my answers (". . . my brother, John"). Ah, how times change—he doesn't even rate in the top 10 anymore. The most humorous sentence on the survey reads, "When I grow up, I want to be . . . [my answer] "a passenger on a train." Shortly thereafter, my mother made sure to take me on a short jaunt on Amtrak, which I loved. Rolling and bouncing along the tracks feels . . . cool.

Train rides evoke a feeling of importance and power. If you're on a train, you've got time. Time to look out the window and take in the changing landscape, time to talk to a stranger next to you or rest your head on the shoulders of the one you love as you listen to the clickety-clack of the train.

Step by Step

10 A.M. (call ahead for specific times): Book a morning ride on the Cuyahoga Valley Scenic Railroad Line. On this historic railway, you can experience what it was like to travel through Ohio when trains were a regular mode of getting from one end of the state to the other in the late 1930s and early 1940s. The coaches on the line were originally built for service on the New York Central and Santa Fe railroads, and they retain so much classic charm that you expect Cary Grant to be sitting next to you.

NOON: The line offers stops in Peninsula, Boston Township, Hale Farm and Village, and Indian Mound. Book your passage farther along the line to visit Stan Hywet Hall and NatureRealm, a 60-room mansion that has the distinction of being the largest Tudor-style house in America. But at the first sight of this home built by Frank Seiberling, founder of the Goodyear Tire & Rubber Company, you'll swear it's a castle. This castle was also home to John Seiberling, grandson to the wealthy rubber baron. It was John Seiberling who fought fiercely to have the Cuyahoga Valley National Recreation Area designated as a national park, and strolling through the gardens at the Seiberling Mansion you'll understand his passion for the area.

The celebrated gardens on the grounds of the mansion stretch out before you, enticing you on a walk through a fragrant blanket of color. Inside, the mansion holds treasures brought here from visiting heads of state from all over the world, artifacts collected by the Seiberlings, and picture-perfect decor that only their distinctive brand of "rubber" checks could buy. Also on the grounds is a concert hall dedicated to providing a year-round schedule of classical and contemporary music.

The coaches on the line were originally built for service on the New York Central and Santa Fe railroads, and they retain so much classic charm that you expect Cary Grant to be sitting next to you.

After you've taken in all the sights and sounds of this place, return to the train for the trip home, possibly planning your next trip on this historic line.

Variations

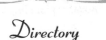

THE HOLIDAY LINE: At Halloween you can ride the Cuyahoga Valley line into "Pumpkin Pandemonium." But the most treasured trips happen at Christmastime, with the "Christmas Tree Adventure." Your train ride will chug you past the frozen, snow-covered route to the town of Peninsula, where you can visit Heritage Farms and pick out a picture-perfect tree. Don't worry, the staff will bundle it up for the ride home, so you won't need to purchase an extra seat for this new addition to your household. Make a point of starting this romantic tradition this season.

Directory

**Cuyahoga Valley
Scenic Railroad**

7600 Riverview Rd., Cleveland

440-526-7128

HOURS/AVAILABILITY:
Call ahead for
reservation and times

**Stan Hywet Hall
and Gardens**

714 N. Portage Path, Akron

330-836-5533

HOURS/AVAILABILITY:
Late-Jan–Mar: Tue–Sat
10 a.m.–4 p.m.,
Sun 1 p.m.–4 p.m.;
April 1–first week of Jan:
grounds open daily
9 a.m.–6 p.m., tours daily
10 a.m.–4:30 p.m.

Outing 49
WALKIN' THE DOG

Season: Spring, Summer, Fall
Time: 2 hours ~ **Location:** West
Intimacy level: 1 ~ **Cost:** $
Advance planning: None

What You'll Do

❧ Leash the dog, grab an iced mocha, and take a stroll down Lake Road ($5).

❧ Play with the pooch at Bradstreet's Landing.

A friend of mine had a serious crush on a very shy guy. She kept trying to think of non-intrusive ways to get the two of them out together for a "non-date kind of date." This went on for weeks until she realized that they both had dogs. They decided to go walking the dogs together, establishing, finally, an ice-breaker. Like these two, stop thinking of walking the dog as a chore and turn it into an adventure. Making a practice of an evening walk together—the three of you—will enhance life for all three of you. Exercise, fresh air, and a satisfied canine will keep you in shape and involved with the outside world.

Step by Step

7 P.M.: Park the car at Cravings parking lot and grab an iced mocha for your walk. Cravings has a wide selection of iced teas, iced and hot coffees, and pastries to choose from, but their mochas—not too sweet and not too tart—are the real draw here.

From Cravings, head west on Lake Road toward Bradstreet's Landing, a healthy one-mile walk. Along the way, do some fantasy house shopping as you pass by the stone and brick homes that make up this exclusive neighborhood. On evenings in the summertime, Lake Road is a favorite spot for neighbors out walking, running, cycling, or roller-blading, and most of the time they'll nod a hello your way. Your dog will enjoy brief visits with neighborhood pups out on their own evening walks, but nothing will surpass his happiness when you arrive at Bradstreet's Landing.

As Snoopy understands all too well, many parks post a "No Dogs Allowed" sign at the front entrance. This is bad news for dogs, who like parks very much. This is not the case here, where dogs are welcome. Though you're strongly encouraged to keep your dog on his leash, many people let their dogs loose to play with other dogs and to take the inevitable swim in the lake. Couples throw sticks or tennis balls into the waves, their dogs rushing happily in to play a game of aquatic catch. Bradstreet's also has a fishing pier, and some dogs like to run the length of the pier and practice their dives. Shore-bound dog owners trade dog stories as they watch their dogs play.

Once your dog has had enough, make sure to leash him and head back home along Lake Road. After completing the second leg of this two-mile walk around dusk, you might be able to talk yourself into a scone or an oversized cookie at Cravings—and grab a bottled water for Scruffy, he's probably thirsty by now.

Variations:

FOR THE DOGLESS: If you like dogs but don't own one, you can still enjoy canine company every once in a while. The Animal Protection

Your dog will enjoy brief visits with neighborhood pups out on their own evening walks, but nothing will surpass his happiness when you arrive at Bradstreet's Landing.

League places dogs in caring homes—saving them from euthanasia. But while they wait for adoption, they still need exercise and human contact. The APL encourages caring souls to participate in their Volunteer Dog Walker program. Simply stop in, fill out a volunteer form, and take a dog or two for a walk around the grounds. The dog is happy, and so are the two of you. It's a great way to spend time with a dog if you can't—or don't want to—own one.

Directory

Animal Protective League
1729 Wiley Ave., Cleveland
216-771-4616
HOURS/AVAILABILITY:
Mon–Fri 11 a.m.–7 p.m.,
Sat 9 a.m.–7 p.m.,
Sun 10 a.m.–4 p.m.

Cravings
19825 Lake Rd., Rocky River
440-331-1191
HOURS/AVAILABILITY:
Mon–Thu 6:30 a.m.–11 p.m.,
Fri–Sat 6:30 a.m.–midnight,
Sun 7:30 a.m.–10 p.m.

Outing 50
GO FLY A KITE!

Season: Spring, Summer, Fall
Time: 2–3 hours ~ **Location:** West
Intimacy level: 1 ~ **Cost:** $
Advance Planning: None

What You'll Do

❧ Watch the kite flyers of Edgewater Park.

❧ Indulge in a potluck picnic.

NOTE: *Plan this outing for the Second Sunday of the month at noon, when the kite flyers congregate at Edgewater Park.*

Kite flying was an Easter Sunday tradition in our family. Each year the Easter Basket would come with a paper kite, and we'd run down to the basement to find just the right rags to attach to the bottom of the kite for ballast while our father constructed the kite to specification. Across the street to the park we'd go, running along with the diamond-shaped object, waiting for just the right moment to release it into flight. It takes two to fly a kite, to enjoy the thrill while it flies—and, well, someone's got to run after the thing when it falls. Thrill yourselves with an afternoon of sharing these duties as colors fly brilliantly above.

On the second Sunday of every month around noon (although members can be seen there just about every week—even in the winter), the Ohio Society for the Elevation of Kites meets at Edgewater Park. This is the group responsible for the colorful streamers and sheets that dance and jolt against the sky at Edgewater Park. The friendly society members—there are currently 75—encourage newcomers. It's worth the trip just to see the sight, but joining in is what it's all about.

The society will help you construct a kite from scratch or walk you through the instructions on a new kite. They'll even let you fly one of theirs for a bit, if you promise not to let go.

"Every year in September we put on the Cleveland Kite Festival," says the society's membership chairman, Elaine Lockhart. "But mostly we meet down at Edgewater—young, old, retired—to fly kites."

A small group of members meets every New Year's Day to fly kites at Edgewater. Though this Polar Bear Club of the Skies is a bit extreme for Lockhart's taste, she admits they have quite a bit of fun with it.

The lake provides a healthy breeze for kite-launching, but any open space will do, especially in the changing, hefty winds of spring and fall. All you need is an open space and a kite.

Directory

Edgewater Park

8107 Lakeshore Blvd. (office), Cleveland

216-881-8141 (office)

HOURS/AVAILABILITY:
Daily dusk–dawn

Outing 51

WARM YOUR HEART OUT IN THE COLD

Season: Winter

Time: 4 hours ~ **Location:** West

Intimacy level: 1 ~ **Cost:** $$

Advance planning: None

What You'll Do

- Get outfitted with skis, boots, and poles ($15 per person).
- Ski the bridle path trail at the Metroparks.
- Munch on wings and pub food.

Keeping your heart in shape is important for love—it's tough to break a heart that's in good shape . . . right? Cross-country skiing is not only a fabulous way to maintain cardiovascular fitness, it's also a challenging way to spend time with your partner in the midst of winter's lovely show. It's easy, too. A few minutes and you're into the rhythm of cross-country skiing, working your arms and legs in constant motion, gliding over the newly fallen snow. But best of all, it's cheap. Developing a cross-country habit is much less costly than a downhill addiction. With no long trips to take, no hotel stays to pay for, and no lift tickets to buy, you can ski cross country on the spur of the moment for under 20 smackers. Fitness, fun, and togetherness at a fair price—why are you hibernating??

Step by Step

1 P.M.: The Wilderness Shop can outfit you with boots, skis, and poles. Catering to a serious outdoor crowd, this store is great for finding additional outdoor gear you might need, from high-tech fiber mittens to water-resistant camping gear. Take advantage of the knowledgeable staff to find everything you need to become an avid cross-country skier.

While you're there, ask the staff about the Metroparks trails. Because they rent skis daily to local customers, they should have a good read on which trails are the best to use and which ones you might want to avoid.

1:30 P.M.: Three areas of the Rocky River Reservation have marked trails for cross-country skiers, but for this outing, try the Little Met Golf Course first. Located just past the Lorain Road Bridge (you can't miss this high, wide bridge above you), the course follows the golf course paths with gentle slopes through wooded areas and follows the Rocky River for a bit. Picnic areas abound if you need a rest, and the area is generally populated with some winter walkers and other skiers—so you won't feel lonely. Cross-country skiing can be strenuous, so pace yourself along the way. Slow down or rest if you feel tired, and try to simply to enjoy the journey.

3 P.M.: Return your skis at the Wilderness Shop and walk next door on Detroit Road to Around the Corner. By now you should have a

A few minutes and you're into the rhythm
of cross-country skiing, working your
arms and legs in constant motion,
gliding over the newly fallen snow.

hearty appetite, and this favorite neighborhood pub will deliver. With its hardwood floors, warm lighting, and high booths, Around the Corner is a great place to warm up after a chilly day. In the afternoon, when it's not crowded, this place is reminiscent of a rustic New England Inn. The menu, full of pub food, features hot Buffalo wings. Order a few dozen along with a piled-high sandwich or a hot bowl of soup. Neighborhood characters amble in and out of the place making plans for the evening while the wait staff trades stories about customers. Sip on ale or order a mug of hot tea while you wait for your food to arrive. Outside, the snow should be accumulating on the old-fashioned windowpanes of Around the Corner. Pat yourself on the back for a hard day's work and know that your hearts grew closer today.

Directory

Around the Corner
18616 Detroit Ave., Lakewood
216-521-4413
HOURS/AVAILABILITY:
Mon–Fri 3 p.m.–2 a.m.,
Sat–Sun 4 p.m.–2 a.m.

Rocky River Reservation
24000 Valley Pkwy., North Olmsted
216-351-6300
HOURS/AVAILABILITY:
Daily dawn–dusk

Wilderness Shop
18636 Detroit Ave., Lakewood
216-521-9100
Hours/availability: Mon 11 a.m.–9 p.m., Tue–Fri 10 a.m.–9 p.m., Sat 10 a.m.–6 p.m., Sun noon–5 p.m.

Outing 52
SKYDIVING

Season: Spring, Summer, Fall
Time: All day ~ **Location:** Southeast
Intimacy level: 2 ~ **Cost:** $$$$
Advance planning: Some

What You'll Do

- Take a class at the Cleveland Parachute Center ($140 per person, tandem jumps $175).
- Have lunch.
- Skydive.
- Celebrate your safe return to the ground with dinner in a country roadhouse ($25–$30).

You're willing to go out on a limb for your love ... but now you're being asked to take a dive. Think of the two of you climbing to 3,500 feet, jumping from a plane, soaring through the air, and landing safely back on terra firma. This is the kind of experience that bonds you together, helps to build trust, and gives you something to talk about for years to come.

Step by Step

8 A.M.: Arrive at the Cleveland Parachute Center to begin training for the dive. The training takes you through all aspects of jumping, from how the equipment works to jumping from the plane to landing safely. The course takes the better part of the morning but is worth the time—specifically if you're nervous about jumping. A video details the jump, from looking out of the aircraft at 13,000 feet to soaring through the air, allowing you to preview what a jump is actually like.

After training, eat a light lunch at the facility. You can pack your own lunch or purchase a sandwich from the center. Meanwhile, jumpmaster Bob Gates will gas up the plane and do a final check on your chutes in preparation for the jump. All the equipment you need is provided, including a nifty radio that you'll use to help steer your way to a smooth landing. The center flies two Cessna 185's and a Twin Bonanza. First-time jumpers have two options. The first is a "square static line" jump from 3,500 feet. In this jump the main parachute, which is square-shaped for easier navigation, will be opened for you by use of a static line attached to the aircraft. Tandem parachuting is the other option. In this scheme, even a first-time jumper can jump from 14,000 feet harnessed directly to an experienced skydiving instructor. Tandem jumps allow you free-fall time—and you need only complete 20 minutes of instruction. Safety is first at Cleveland Parachute Center, and every precaution is taken to ensure that the jump is fail-proof and safe.

After completing five such jumps successfully, you can progress to free-fall jumping from 13,000 feet with the goal of free-fall jumping together—the ultimate jump.

Tackling such a physical and mental challenge together will put other problems or hurdles into perspective for the two of you, especially if you have some trepidation before going. Challenge yourselves and stick to it. You might find, like many jumpers do, that it's an addictively thrilling sport.

Think of the two of you climbing to 3,500 feet, jumping from a plane, soaring through the air, and landing safely back on terra firma.

5 P.M.: After your jump, reward yourself with a hearty dinner at J.D.'s Post House. Prime rib is the specialty at the Post House, a restaurant that, from the outside, looks like a country home. Inside, the rustic, familial charm and warmth of the room will put you immediately in a meat-and-potatoes mood. Order the prime rib or a fresh-cut steak with all the trimmings as you talk about your thrilling day over dinner.

Variations:

VIRTUAL JUMPS: In addition to live jumping, the Cleveland Parachute Center is the first in the country to use a 3-D Graphics Virtual Reality Simulator. Originally designed to train the military's special forces, the simulator has the ability to provide a lifelike experience for those afraid of jumping or unable to jump because of age or disability. The 10 minutes you get on the simulator is equal to three jumps from a plane. Cost is only $25 per person.

Directory

Cleveland Parachute Center, Inc.
15199 Grove Rd., Garrettsville
800-852-5867
HOURS/AVAILABILITY:
Call for times.

J.D.'s Post House
16240 Main Market St., Parkman
440-548-2300
HOURS/AVAILABILITY:
Mon–Thu 10:30 a.m.–9 p.m.,
Fri 10:30 a.m.–10 p.m.,
Sat 8 a.m.–10 p.m.,
Sun 8 a.m.–9 p.m.

INDEX

What's So Big About Cleveland, Ohio? / What does a well-traveled 10-year-old think about her first visit to Cleveland? "B-o-o-o-ring". Until, that is, she discovers a very special little secret … *Sara Holbrook & Ennis McNulty* / $17.95 hardcover

Ghoulardi / The behind-the-scenes story of Cleveland's wildest TV legend. Rare photos, interviews, show transcripts, and Ghoulardi trivia. *Tom Feran & R. D. Heldenfels* / $17.95 softcover

The Ghoul Scrapbook / Rare photos, show transcripts, and video captures from "The Main Maniac" of Cleveland late-night TV. *Ron Sweed & Mike Olszewski* / $17.95 softcover

Feagler's Cleveland / The best from three decades of commentary by Cleveland's top columnist, Dick Feagler. Witty, insightful, opinionated, thoughtful. / $13.95 softcover

"Did You Read Feagler Today?" / The most talked about recent columns by Cleveland's most outspoken columnist. / $13.95 softcover

On Being Brown / Thoughtful essays and interviews exploring what it means to be a true fan of the Cleveland Browns. *Scott Huler* / $18.95 hardcover, $10.95 softcover

Indians Memories / A nostalgic roller coaster ride including laughably bad seasons and two exciting eras of championship baseball. *Tim Long* / $5.95 softcover

Barnaby and Me / Linn Sheldon, a Cleveland TV legend as "Barnaby", tells the fascinating story of his own extraordinary life. / $20.00 hardcover

The Great Indoors / The first decade of Eric Broder's hilarious weekly "Great Indoors" column. Reread favorites, or get caught up with the ongoing saga. / $13.95 softcover

Cleveland Sports Trivia Quiz / Test your knowledge with these 500 brain-teasing questions and answers on all kinds of Cleveland sports. *Tim Long* / $6.95 softcover

Cleveland TV Memories / Remember when TV was local? A nostalgic collection of 365 favorite local shows, hosts, jingles, bloopers, stunts, and more. *Feran & Heldenfels* / $6.95 softcover

Bed & Breakfast Getaways from Cleveland / 80 charming small inns perfect for an easy weekend or evening away from home. *Doris Larson* / $13.95 softcover

The Cleveland Orchestra Story / How a midwestern orchestra became a titan in the world of classical music. With 102 rare photographs. *Donald Rosenberg* / $40.00 hardcover

Available at your local bookstore.

These books are stocked at Northeast Ohio bookstores, are available through most online book retailers, and can be ordered at any bookstore in the U.S.

Need help finding a retailer near you? Call us: 1-800-915-3609.

Gray & Company, Publishers
1588 E. 40th St., Cleveland, OH 44103 / 216-431-2665
www.grayco.com